Moon Rock

Mare Crisium

by Thad Roberts

Moon Rock: Mare Crisium
By Thad Roberts

First Edition

Nonfiction, companion book to *Sex on the Moon* by Ben
Mezrich, followed by *Moon Rock: Mare Tranquillitatis*

Available in softback (Amazon), e-book (Kindle &
iBooks), and audiobook (Audible & iTunes)

First Print Date, January 15, 2018

ISBN 978-0-9963942-5-3

Cover by Jeff Chapple, Derek Meik & Jamie Lombardi

www.moonrockbook.com

Other books by Thad Roberts:
Einstein's Intuition: Visualizing Nature in Eleven
Dimensions
www.EinsteinsInutition.com

"People seem not to see that their opinion of the world is also a confession of character."

~ Ralph Waldo Emerson

FOREWORD

"Okay," he continued, repositioning himself. "If you don't learn what free really is, then some day you're gonna be in prison, under the sun looking up and watching planes going by. And when that day comes you're gonna think to yourself, if only I was on that plane instead of being here, trapped in this place, then I'd be happy. And then one day you'll be out, and you'll end up on one of those planes, flying over people below that are looking up wishing they was somewhere else, in a different life, an important life, going somewhere important. But instead of celebrating that you've made it, and being blissfully happy with your life, you know what you'll be doing when that moment comes? You'll be worried about the meeting you're going to. Will it go well? Am I prepared? Did I impress the right people... The fucking game is the same no matter what level you're on. It's rigged to keep you unhappy, to keep you always looking up and reaching for something else, thinking your shit is just around the corner, just one more promotion, a bigger raise, more power, more money, more respect... It's all fucked. Those people in those planes are just as trapped as you are right now. There's only one way to be free in this world. Only one."

WARNING

If you're going to read this book, and brave following me into prison where the lies we've all grown accustomed to no longer hold their spell, be warned that this is not the fluffy politically correct version of my arrest, or the version watered down by the media for the pallet of the self-righteous. This is the raw truth, what actually happened—the kind of truth that only someone that has been stripped of their ability to pretend that they aren't a fuck up could offer.

Juxtaposed against a world of people whitewashing their internal dialogue before regurgitating it to propel themselves up the pompous ladder, prisoners have to sit with who they actually are. This isolation eventually affords them a chance to cut beneath the surface of expectation, to see past the delusions they once confused for their reflection. If your political affiliations, or religious views, require you to deny that kind of honesty, or demand that you twist the insights that fall out of that process until they look like something you prefer to believe in, consider this your warning, that you'll have your work cut out for you while reading this book.

To save me from being fucked over by anyone that might be upset that I nakedly exposed them to the world, in this coward's world of litigation, I changed some of the names. Other than that, this account is completely true. Like all true stories, everyone in it, despite having positive motivations, is swimming through a world diseased with outmoded traditions, contradictions, and slight of hand manipulations. Although each person tries to navigate that mess in a way that paints meaning into their lives, inevitably, they fuck up, usually in proportion to the hand they were originally dealt. My fuck ups, however, defy that usual relation.

The newspapers will tell you that I was an inspiring astronaut who pulled off the most audacious heist in history, stealing the most valuable substance ever, the moon, or rather moon rocks from NASA, to impress my girlfriend, all for love. Others will tell you that I had sex on the moon with my mistress, while my wife was at home, oblivious. Some of the more flamboyant sources will tell you that the guy that stole the moon was a romantic genius, a lunatic, a science prodigy, or a mastermind manipulator. These stories are all woven together by people grasping at threads of truth in the dark, filling in what's left with flights of fancy patterned through the lens of their own lives.

The national bestseller 'Sex on the Moon', by Ben Mezrich, got the facts right, in a vanilla sort of way, but failed to capture more than a veneer of the internal landscape and motivations behind that infamous act. It also ends where the real transformations begin, where this book picks up.

"Welcome to the real world Moon Rock."

Chapter 1: The Fall

Stepping out of the car, I looked up and took a deep breath under the warm setting sun. This was it. On our deathbeds we would tell our grandchildren about this day. They wouldn't believe us, but we'd tell them anyway, with a thrill in our voice, holding hands as we uttered our lifelong secret aloud. Every day between now and then we'd look into each other's eyes with a knowing smile, connected by this secret celestial bond.

I stood tall and smiled at the poetic timing—exactly thirty-three years from history's most famous step.

As I walked away from the car time began to feel like molasses, slowing down and dragging itself across the nuisances that regularly go unnoticed. Small out of place movements filled my periphery–shadows that didn't belong. Then I noticed a helicopter flying suspiciously low nearby. My heart stopped.

"Put your hands on your head!" yelled a voice behind me.

I spun around. Men in black combat gear were quickly circling in, guns raised, arms tense. Undercover officers, dressed in suits were also glaring at me from behind their guns. They came from everywhere, around the building, behind cars, across the street. They were making their way through the parking lot like a raiding party of ants, eager to tear the flesh of their newest find, fiercely gripping their guns. The helicopter was now directly overhead.

"Put your hands on your head. Now! Do it now!" the voice repeated.

With my heart beating out of my chest, I froze, moving only my eyes, as I watched them advance and encircle me. Then I focused in on the officer right in front of me and glared at him like the present was somehow something I could step outside of.

Passionate memories flashed through my mind, rapidly weaving a patchwork of delightful emotions that cascaded into hopes for the future. I was instantly transported under the stars in the Grand Staircase Escalante National Monument where the Milky Way was so bright that I had a definite shadow on a moonless night. Then I was digging up dinosaur bones with the paleontology crew, unearthing a piece of evolution's hidden story. An instant later I was riding my mountain bike from Salt Lake City to San Francisco to raise money for the Cystic Fibrosis Foundation. Then I was running the observatory and applying for a job at NASA. In the next instant I was captivated, all over again, by the way Tiffany looked in her little black bikini as she jumped off that bridge. Then I was SCUBA diving with astronauts in the Neutral Buoyancy Laboratory around a mock-up of the International Space Station, then back on dry land driving my car while Tiffany read Nietzsche to me, legs folded, her excitement for our joint exploration pouring from her lips.

With each blink of the present the hopes encased by each of those memories were shattered into little shards, cutting me as they poured out from my body into a bottomless, dark abyss. A wave of desperation overcame me. I couldn't just let this happen without a fight. I had to act. Apocryphal Aztec legends played in the background of my mind—tales of the winning team's captain cutting off his own head after winning the celebrated ōllamaliztli ball game so that he might go out in a moment of glory, forever existing inside the only moment capable of cradling the audacity of his true aim.

The tension in their bodies was obvious, wide stances, rigid apathy for the human condition, robotic response to orders. I could feel the story they were telling themselves, feeding the sense of danger that filled the moment, imagining me as a threat large enough to deserve what they were prepared to do. In response, I imagined rushing the officer directly in front of me, meeting his serious gaze and his tightly locked grip on his gun with the exact end he was conjuring. It would all be over soon. All I had to do was lunge.

In the distance, I heard more voices yelling. "Get down on the ground!" But these commands weren't directed at me.

I looked past the formation of rigid callousness that surrounded me, focusing in on Tiffany as she dropped to her knees and then her stomach, spreading out on the asphalt. Two officers rushed up to cuff her hands behind her back.

Keeping the rest of my body frozen, I slowly closed my eyes and saw her in another moment—lying on the bed, penetrating me with eyes that melted the rest of the world away, gyrating her naked body with anticipation. She reached for me, begging me to approach, full of hope and desire, unlocking potential I had not dared unleash.

I reopened my eyes, relaxed my posture and slowly raised my hands.

...

For an hour I sat in a white unmarked van with caged up windows. My hands were cuffed behind my back, slightly digging metal into my wrists. Another set of cuffs chained my feet together at the ankles. I twisted around every couple of minutes, trading between positions that dug the cuffs into my skin and ones that cramped my muscles. All the while my mind was racing, calculating, projecting, wondering how I could possibly fix this. Was it all over?

The more my heart raced, the harder it was to breathe. Looking out the window, ignoring the swarm of cops in the foreground, I looked at the hotel and counted nine flights up and found our room. The memory of her touch comforted me. Her bare skin, the excitement in her eyes, the softness of her lips, the bliss of my hands on her hips, her unending playful energy... our plan. I closed my eyes and desperately tried to return to that moment, but the present was too suffocating.

One of the suits approached the van and signaled a uniformed officer standing just outside it to open the door.

He slid the door open and said, "Get out," in a calm voice.

From the back seat I stretched my legs forward, struggling to figure out how to step down without separating my feet. Frustrated, I just hopped out with both feet at the same time. The man in the suit leaned towards me, grabbed my arm and quietly said, "Don't ever say that I didn't do anything for you."

He used his key to unlock one of my restraints then re-cuffed my hands together in front of me. Then he grabbed my arm again and started walking me across the parking lot. The place was still swarming with cops, but they weren't nearly as serious as before, just walking around like actual people doing regular tasks.

Two cops followed us. My eyes were darting everywhere, trying to notice every detail, desperate to find something that would count as a clue. Near the hotel entrance my escort directed me to a white unmarked car. He opened the back door and signaled with a nod for me to get in.

"You got five minutes," he said.

I awkwardly bent over, sat down and then swung my legs inside the car.

Tiffany was in the middle of the bench seat, looking slightly away. Tracks of tears ran down her face. Two officers were sitting in the front seats pretending that they weren't observing us.

"Are you okay?" I asked as I leaned towards her gaze. Her eyes met mine and she began to gush.

"I told them everything," she said. "I'm sorry. I told them everything." The tears poured out of her, and her beautiful, petite body was shivering. I reached up and awkwardly tried to wipe her tears with my cuffed hands.

"You don't have anything to be sorry about," I said. Her eyes were red from crying.

"This ruins everything," she said.

I put my hands on her leg and let her feel my presence. We held each other, closing our eyes, trying to caress the nightmare away.

The police radio started squawking, breaking the spell. I pulled back and looked into her eyes. "I love you," I said.

"I love you too," she said, finally looking me in the eyes.

I squeezed her leg a little, quickly glanced at the two cops in front and then, in a soft but serious timbre, I said, "Anything you have to do..."

She nodded, trying to keep it together.

I desperately tried to absorb her, to disappear into this moment of touch, but it slipped through my grip and joined the ever-receding flow of time.

"Just don't forget to write me," I said, no longer able to keep my tears back.

"I won't," she assured.

She tried to wipe my tears with soft trembling hands. I dove into the depths of her textured blue eyes, remembering the future we had dared to dream of, trying to hold onto the safety of the world fortified in our union.

We cried, softly kissing each other.

"I don't know what to do," she said completely losing her composure again.

With my mouth close to her ear I softly said, "You do everything you can to live a full and happy life. And if I go away for a long time then you date, and laugh," I paused for a moment, "and love."

She pulled away a little, started to shake her head, but then caught my eyes.

I continued, "The universe needs you to be happy, my love. I need to know that you're happy, that you're exploring the world like you always do, that you're laughing and talking French in bed."

She interrupted, "I just barely got used to not being alone in bed, and now I have to learn how to be alone again."

My door opened and the officer said, "Its time."

"They're saying we could get five to ten years for this," she said.

I looked in her eyes and said, "That's not going to happen."

She put her hands on mine and said, "I love you."

"You're going to be okay," I said. "I promise."

"Let's go!" the officer said.

"I can survive as long as you write me," I said, choking up.

I started to scoot out, still looking at her. She raised her hands, looked at her cuffs and then back at me and said, "Kind of ruins the fantasy, doesn't it?"

We cried and laughed at the same time.

. . .

The door slammed behind me, echoing between the cement walls. In the last two days, there had been six different holding cells with only subtle differences. I was barely able to walk, exhausted with sleep deprivation. There were five other men in the holding cell and it was freezing cold. The man farthest to the left was pacing back and forth between the stainless steel toilet-sink and the door.

"Fuck man. Fuck. My ol' lady is going to kill me," he said talking to himself.

He was thin, had scraggly brown hair covering his ears, and was clasping his hands behind his back, twitching his interlocked fingers as if he were playing his knuckles like a piano.

The fluorescent lights flickered, partially dimming the room in a nauseating way. The other four men were sitting on the cement bench that jutted out of the back and right walls. Closest to the toilet-sink was a black man, average height, a bit overweight, with his hair twisted into a scattering of little spikes. His elbows were on his knees with his face planted in his hands, eyes closed.

Next to him was an obese white man that was breathing loudly through his open mouth and looking right at me in a way that made me uneasier than I already was.

In the corner, a Mexican in his early thirties was in an upright fetal position with his feet up on the bench, knees tucked into his chest. He was leaning forward and rubbing his legs in an attempt to get warm. He briefly glanced at me and then quickly returned to watching the pacer.

A black man with cornrowed hair in his early twenties was sitting closest to the door, furiously twitching one leg. He was playing with a roll of toilet paper in his hands, like it was a football, staring right at me. We were all dressed in plastic flip-flops with no socks and bright red jumpsuits.

"They're going to tow the car. I know it. They're going to tow the car. Fuck!" the pacer said.

I sat down between the Mexican and the young black man and quickly found out why my spot had been left unoccupied. The vent in the ceiling was blowing cold air into the room, right in this direction. I scanned the cell, over and over, desperately hoping that a warm bed would appear.

The mouth breather was still looking at me. The cement was cold, much colder than I expected. It quickly drained the heat from my body making me increasingly sensitive to the cold air blowing from the ceiling vent. I pulled my legs to my chest, attempting to stay warm and closed my eyes for a minute, trying to block out the flickering lights.

"Fuck man, Fuck!" the pacer exclaimed. "Stupid… can't believe how fuck'n stupid." His flip-flops were dragging on the floor as he walked, loudly echoing through the room. The mouth breather interrupted his regular rhythm with a startling snort.

After about twenty minutes of ceaseless mumbling the pacer loudly exclaimed, "Fuck, this don't make no sense!" He walked to the door, looked out the little square plastic window and yelled, "Why is this taking so long?"

"Muthafucka! Shut the fuck up," Pudgy said as he broke his statue pose. "I been down foe three years and den some, got six moe to go, and your punk ass is getting out tomorrow, worried about yo hoe and yo wheels? Pfffff, muthafucka, sit down and shut the fuck up."

"Uh huh, that's what I'm saying," Cornrows added in support.

The pacer stopped moving but didn't sit down. Several minutes later, we heard the sound of keys. Cornrows got up and watched out the window. The pacer stared at the door intensely. As the jingling keys approached, Cornrows quickly backed out of sight, trying to hide from the officer. We heard the sound of a door opening, but it wasn't our door. A few seconds later we heard it slam shut, followed by the clanking of keys fading into the distance.

The pacer started up his moving rant again.

"What the fuck man. The fuck they doing out

there?" he said.

Cornrows went back in front of the small Plexiglas window and pounded on it like it was an hourglass whose flow rate depended on his agitation. Something caught his attention. He went quiet and glued his face to the portal. A few minutes later he started yelling.

"Hey shortie, holla!"

He was getting excited, staying up on his tiptoes to get a better view.

"Show me dem titties girl." He paused for a couple of seconds and then yelled, "Dem titties!" He shook his right hand to emphasize his words, still holding the roll of toilet paper in his left.

He was smiling from ear to ear, constantly shifting his weight from one leg to the next. Just then an officer appeared on the other side of the glass. Cornrows jumped back.

"Damn boss, why you got to sneak up on me like dat?" he said.

Without saying a word, the officer swung a metallic cover over the window.

I could tell I wasn't the only one that hadn't slept in over two days. There was no clock, but my body told me that it was definitely past midnight. We all tried to find a position that was comfortable enough to fall asleep, but the air conditioning was far too cold.

I was sitting down on the floor, as far away as I could get from the source of the cold air. I tried to rest my head on my knees, keeping my back from touching the wall, but I couldn't fall asleep in that position. I tried lying on my back, but the hard ground quickly sucked all the heat out of me, especially when my head was directly on the cement. I had to get up and move around to warm back up. Next, I tried lying on my side, but I just couldn't get comfortable enough to sleep without something to put under my head.

...

Cornrows was the only one getting any sleep. He was on his side on the floor, resting his head on the roll of toilet paper.

"Hey nigga," Pudgy said.

Cornrows didn't respond.

"Hey nigga!" Pudgy said more forcefully.

"What?" Cornrows said as he opened one eye.

"I gotta take a shit."

"So?"

"So... I need that roll nigga. What you think?"

Cornrows closed his eye and didn't move.

"Hey nigga!" Pudgy said more loudly. "Don't make me come over there and smack you upside the head."

Cornrows kept his eyes closed and said, "Shit ol man, you gots a glass jaw like all the rest."

"Muthafucka," Pudgy said. He stood up and added, "I gots to drop a deuce nigga. You can either give me that roll, or I can drop it right here."

"Fuck man," Cornrows said as he sat up and tossed the roll to Pudgy.

We couldn't get away from the sounds as he sat on

the toilet. All we could do was close our eyes and try not to breathe.

"Agua, agua," Cornrows said.

Pudgy flushed the toilet in response. Then again, and again.

When he was done he flushed one last time and then returned to his spot on the bench. Laying down on his side, he placed his head on the toilet roll. Cornrows looked at him and said, "Ah hell naw nigga. Give it here muthafucka," as he jerked his head to the side.

"You had your turn nigga. Time for someone else to get some sleep," Pudgy replied.

"Hell naw muthafucka, that's my muthafuckin' roll dawg. I snatched it soon as I came up in here," Cornrows said.

"Look muthafucka," Pudgy said as he repositioned the roll beneath his head, "a nigga gots to sleep. If you want this roll you can have it, but I'm laying my muthafuckin' head on your feets." He relaxed into his new position and began closing his eyes.

Cornrows stood up, puffing up his chest and breathing fast. Pudgy kept his eyes closed, and said, "Ain't nothin' personal nigga. I'm just saying, muthafucka gots to get some sleep up in here. Feel me?"

Cornrows stood there for a while, making fists and curling his lips. Finally he said, "Shiiiit, give it here."

Pudgy opened his eyes, slowly sat up and stared Cornrows down for a few seconds, ascertaining the commitment behind their new contract. Cornrows sat down in the middle of the cement floor and held out his hands. Pudgy threw the roll of toilet paper to him. Cornrows got down on his side with his knees tucked towards his chest and placed the roll under his head. Pudgy got down next to him, shifting around to find the best position and then put his head on Cornrows' ankles. Then, without saying a word, the mouth breather followed suit, resting his head on Pudgy's legs. The Mexican followed, then I followed.

...

I opened my eyes and felt the full color of my life come rushing back in. I let out a sigh of relief. "It was only a bad dream," I whispered to myself. Delighting in my great fortune, I took a deep breath and pulled her naked body closer to mine. Lost in the warmth of her skin, I began caressing her, tracing out her feminine curves with my fingers. Her body slowly moved with her breath, growing more and more intense. I kissed the back of her neck and her shoulders, and after roaming around for a while, my hands softly landed on her hips and gripped firmly. She arched her back invitingly pushing herself towards me as her breath quickened.

My heart was racing, overwhelmed with the softness of her skin, the feel of her hair on my lips and her flowery smell. I wanted to tell her how happy I was that it was only a dream, that she was here with me instead, but I didn't want to breath any more life into that nightmare than it had already taken.

I slid one hand to her breast and pulled her tightly into me, nibbling on the nape of her neck, feeling her rise. She was breathing even faster. I reached down to feel her wetness and felt her whole body quiver with anticipation. I grabbed my cock and placed it just outside, teasing her before I pushed in.

Suddenly, a violent jolt beneath my head tore her away from me. Her warmth and softness transformed into a world of cold hard cement and a Mexican pillow that twitched with night terrors. I slowly opened my eyes, hoping not to see myself playing the caboose of an awkward daisy chain of strange men. "Fuck," I sighed.

The mouth breather was now rhythmically snoring. Silence, followed by a desperate gasp of air and a loud snort, followed by a vibrating exhale, over and over and over. It was unbearably annoying, like a jackhammer chiseling a reminder right into my skull that everything that mattered in my life was all over.

For the next twenty minutes I tried to fall back asleep, but every time I started to relax, or block out the rush of my mind and ignore the cold, another loud snort from the mouth breather echoed throughout the chamber triggering a twitch in the Mexican's legs. I gave up and returned to sitting in my own upright fetal position on the cement bench.

CHAPTER 2: THE SUBMARINE

卌 ||||

Maybe it was a joke, put up there by an officer with a flair for scurrilous humor, but it looked official. Right in the middle of the archway, a plaque rich with subtext proudly marked the entrance of our new, poorly lit dungeon. It read, "Abandon all hope, ye who enter here."

Our chains clinked partially in sync with the lead officer's keys as they walked us down an inclined concrete ramp through a steel-walled hallway leading into the bowels of Morgan Street jail.

"They call this place the submarine," the guy next to me said.

"Why is that?" I asked.

"You'll see," he said.

Each of us was awkwardly carrying a bedroll between our arms, despite the cuffs around our wrists.

As we descended, echoes of muffled screaming got louder. Flickering and humming fluorescent bulbs were separated by long stretches down the hallway. The darkness between lights made the shuffling of our plastic sandals on polished cement sound louder.

The guard in the front stopped beneath the first strobe light. "Hold it," he said. We stopped and watched as he fiddled through his ring of oversized keys and then inserted one that was about six inches long into a metallic slot on the left wall.

The key opened a small box full of levers with round black knobs. The guard pumped some of the levers and then left one in the down position. A metallic door electronically recessed into the wall. Unnatural light poured into the corridor.

The second guard stared at his clipboard under the noxious, alien glare. Then, in competition with the all-pervasive electric drone, he yelled "Brown, oh one six." One of the prisoners stepped forward hugging his bedroll composed of two blankets, a sheet, and a pillowcase. One guard checked his plastic ID wristband and scratched his name off the list as the other removed his chains. With a nod, the guard with the keys directed the prisoner to go inside. He stepped forward and then turned around and watched the door grind closed behind him.

The rest of us shuffled our way further down the hall. The officer called out another number under the next flickering light. The man that had informed me of the name of this place stepped up. After his cuffs were removed, he stepped inside without looking back. Further down the corridor it was my turn. Once my chains were off and my number crossed off the list, I stepped inside my new dungeon. I froze as the steel door closed behind me, disoriented by the shrill of Jacob's ladder pulses that emanated from every light bulb, each with its own choppy rhythm.

I was in a small vestibule that separated two rooms. On the right, the so-called 'day room', there were two metal tables with metallic stools attached, bolted to the ground. The back wall consisted of only bars, with an antique payphone attached to them near the left side of the room, the kind that took collect calls only. Near the ceiling, in the farthest corner, a small television with poor reception was blaring. No one was watching it.

There was only one prisoner in this room, a black man sitting in the corner beneath the television, next to the wall of bars. He didn't look at me. He was hugging his knees, rocking side to side, as if he was attempting to get his consciousness to slip into nothingness.

The room on the left—the 'night room'—contained six metal bunk beds permanently fixed in place, two mop buckets, one mop, two metal toilets with no toilet seats, a metal sink with pump buttons, and a shower in the space that separated the two rooms.

Four men were sitting on two adjacent bottom bunks, facing each other and playing cards. Four other men were lying in their bunks. They weren't sleeping. Three of them were just blinking into the flickering noisy lights. The other had his hands pressed to his ears with his elbows up and his eyes closed.

One of the card players jumped up suddenly. "What muthafucka? What!" he said as he slapped a card down on the floor face up between the bunks. He was tall, maybe six foot three, with broad shoulders, had a patchy beard and his head was patterned with rows of short little twisted spikes that grew larger from one side of his head to the other.

Two white men, one fat and white-haired and one young and wiry, were both sitting on a bottom bunk looking at me.

Another player, in his late twenties, with a prominent gold tooth and tattoos on his neck, was sitting on the edge of the bed shaking both legs furiously and intensely fixating on the pile of cards on the floor. Suddenly he stood up, raised his card high over his head and slapped it on the floor yelling, "That's what I'm talkin' bout muthafucka. That's what I'm talkin' bout."

Only one bunk was vacant, an upper bunk in the center row near the wall furthest from the cell entrance. I approached the empty bunk, tied my sheet and one of the thin gray blankets around the green plastic mattress, then neatly folded the other blanket and tightly tucked it in around the foot of the mattress.

Another one of the card players excitedly yelled, "What ya gonna do, huh? What ya gonna do?" He stood up, shifting his weight back and forth from one leg to the next, leaning forward, taunting the other player.

I slipped out of my plastic sandals, stepped on the frame of the lower bunk, trying not to touch the lower bunk mattress, and climbed up. Exhausted, I laid down on top of the covers.

After a few minutes of stretching out I sat up, unbuttoned my issued coveralls, removed the white t-shirt, and stuffed my pillowcase with it. It was a bit lumpy, but it made lying on my side much easier. Finally able to get comfortable in that position, I curled up in an attempt to stay warm.

"I wouldn't do that," the young white kid said in a voice loud enough to overcome the buzz of the lights. I looked up at him.

"Do what?" I asked.

He responded with a slight head gesture while shifting his eyes to my pillow.

"What do you mean?" I asked.

"Ain't nothing s'posed to be in our sacks," he explained.

Trying to gauge whether or not he was being serious, I looked around and noticed that all of the pillowcases in the room were empty.

"Well then what's the point of having pillowcases?" I asked.

Without looking up from his card game the older man, who looked a lot like Santa, chuckled a bit and said, "To remind you that you don't have a pillow of course."

I put my shirt back on and resumed trading back and forth between a relatively warm position and one that didn't kink my neck.

After a few minutes of tossing around I sat up and leaned towards the Kid. "What will they do if I get under my cover?" I asked.

"Try it and find out," he said. "But if they shake us down and take my cards or any of my shit, you're gonna pay me back," he said. Santa's face didn't flinch. I looked around and saw that the other men on their bunks were curled up, trying to stay as warm as possible without getting under their covers. I laid back down and covered my ears in an attempt to keep my mind off the buzzing, which by now was beginning to push deep into my consciousness. It was a useless endeavor.

"Chingado", one of the black men said as he sat up and went to the toilet. He pulled down his jumpsuit, and sat down on the toilet in full sight of us all.

"Agua, agua", one of the card players called out immediately.

Several others chimed in without flinching or even moving their heads. "Agua, agua."

The man on the toilet contorted himself and pushed the small round metallic button mounted in the wall behind him. The flush was loud. Seconds later he dropped his hand back to his side and several people immediately yelled out, "Agua, agua".

He flushed again, but this time left his hand on the button. The chanting stopped.

After he was done shitting, he returned to his bunk. Then the man from the day room entered the night room and sat on the bottom bunk adjacent to mine. He pulled something out of his pants and arranged himself on his bunk. I tried to see what he was doing without making it too obvious that I was looking. He had folded his cover down just beneath where he was sitting and was apparently methodologically tearing his sheet into little long strips and braiding them together.

The black man above him leaned over the side of his bunk and hoarsely whispered something in Spanish that I couldn't understand. He continued tearing his sheet without responding. I laid down under the flickering lights and tried to hold onto any thought that carried me away from here, but the noxious buzzing stole all my chances to escape, screeching in my ears and pounding in my head.

...

"Chow time, chow time, chow time," an officer yelled over the speakers. The man braiding his sheet stuffed his progress back into his pants, got out of his bed, then straightened out his remaining sheet and neatly arranged his cover on top of it.

After a few minutes, an officer banged on our door and opened the rectangular slot in it. We all lined up and took our turns showing our thick plastic wrist ID's through the slot and proceeded to grab the brown plastic tray of food that was pushed through the hole. The trays were thick and sturdy with different sectioned compartments for corn bread, some kind of brown porridge-looking goop, and a spoonful of broth soup.

One by one, we sat down at the tables in the day room. An Evangelical preacher, dressed in an expensive suit, was playing the crowd on the TV. One of the Spanish speaking men began searching for something better to watch. He was in his mid-thirties and had so little body fat that his face was just bone with skin tightly stretched over it. He scanned through several channels of fuzzy snow until he came to the only other channel that came in clearly–the Teletubbies. He walked backwards to his seat with his eyes glued to the screen. As he ate, he laughed with excitement every time the colorful antennae blobs danced.

The rest of us ate without talking, ignoring the TV, pushing our cheap plastic sporks into each square hoping for something solid to push back. When the first man finished scraping up the last bit of his food, he left his tray on the table and went into the night room. Everyone else finished eating but stayed in the day room waiting.

The volume was turned up all the way on the TV in an attempt to compete with the buzzing lights, and the high pitch competition was giving me a headache. When the advertisements came on, Skeletor got up and approached the unaccompanied tray. He looked it over with great interest for a few seconds and then returned to his seat.

After a couple of minutes, the man in the next room returned and sat back down with a blank stare. Someone else got up and went to the next room. When he returned, the guy sitting next to me tapped me on the shoulder and said something I couldn't quite make out. I turned and watched his mouth as he talked.

"Do you have to go?" he asked. I looked at him with confusion. "Shit," he said as he pointed to the next room.

"Oh, no thanks," I said. "Go ahead." He left his tray behind.

Ten minutes later the guard yelled, "Trays!" as he opened the slot in our door. We each slid our empty tray through. Everyone went back to their routine, sitting for hours, trying to block out the loud buzzing of the lights, or playing Hearts.

The rhythm of my new world was jarring and disorienting.

"Dats right, dats right, dats right," the player with a scar from his left ear to his nose yelled with excitement as he tossed the jack of hearts to the floor. "Time to bleed muthafuckas, time to bleed!" The next player threw out the seven of hearts, followed by the ten of hearts and the nine of hearts.

"Dats what I'm talking about," Scarface said as he bobbed his head. He took the hand and then threw down the ace of hearts. "Now where's my bitch?

After that round, he scooped up the cards and threw out the king of hearts. "Dat's what I'm talk'n bout, dats what I'm talk'n bout!" he exclaimed. The next player played the three of hearts, followed by the queen of spades. "Dats right niggas, dats right niggas, dis nigga's bout to school all y'all muthafuckas," Scarface said.

The player with a teardrop tattoo on his upper left cheek chimed in. "Talk is cheap nigga, talk is cheap." He looked like he was permanently squinting and clenching his jaw.

The last player in the round discarded a two of hearts and Scarface proudly scooped up the hand. Next he threw out a five of clubs, which was followed by the three of clubs, the ace of clubs, and the two of clubs. Teardrop picked the hand off the floor in a deliberately slow display.

"Dat's ok nigga, dats ok, we still sweeping the floor up in here," Scarface said as he sat on the very edge of the bunk shaking his legs. Teardrop started the next hand with the eight of hearts. Scarface immediately stood up and towered over Teardrop. "Hell naw muthafucka. Come on nigga, you gonna play me like dat? Huh, you gonna play me like dat?" He threw the six of hearts on the floor, turning around and yelling, "muthafucka." Teardrop collected the hand and set aside the two hearts.

As the card game continued, one of the black men got off his bunk and dropped his coveralls to his waist, tying the arms around him like a belt. Then he removed his T-shirt and placed it on the ground in front of him. Reaching beneath the folded cover at the foot of his bed he pulled out a deck of cards. He shuffled the deck several times like a magician, breathing deeply as he rolled his shoulders back and forth.

When he was satisfied with the deck he placed it on his bunk and flipped the top card over. It was the seven of clubs. He lowered himself to the ground, placed his hands on his shirt, carefully stretching it to some exact memorized spacing, then did seven push-ups. Then he stood back up and flipped the next card. It was the jack of diamonds. Back on the floor, he arranged his hands just right on the shirt and did ten push-ups. He went through the entire deck like this.

I approached Santa's bunk and asked, "How do I get a deck of cards?"

"You can order them on commissary," Santa said. "Oh," I said as I looked down. "But they don't let you take them with you when you transfer," Santa added. "So if you just wait around long enough you'll get some." He reached under his mattress and grabbed a well-used deck. "Here, until then you can use this one."

"Thanks, I said." I climbed onto my top bunk, sat cross-legged and began playing Solitaire.

After I had completed two games Santa slowly stood up with his hands on his back and then approached my bunk. "Do you got anyone out there looking out for you?" he asked. I didn't respond.

"Wife? Parents? Friends?"

I stopped playing, but didn't look at him.

"You can keep the cards," he said.

After watching me play for a few minutes he asked, "So what you in here for?" I felt he pit in my stomach sprout out with his words, paralyzing me in the feeling of abandonment I had been trying to distract myself from.

"Wait, wait, let me guess," he said with enthusiasm. "It was a girl right?" He noticed that I hesitated with my cards. "It's always a girl," he added.

"Tax evasion," the Kid chimed in.

"No, not taxes," Santa said. He studied my face. "You were going for the big time right? Something to impress... maybe pull off some scheme to get millions of dollars, be the big man, but then when you made it, it wasn't enough, was it?"

I stopped playing and looked at him. "I definitely

never 'made it'," I said.

"Nobody ever feels like they made it college boy... it's something you can only see from below," he replied.

"Oh oh oh," the Kid added. "Did you pull off one of them computer scams, where you take little bits of money from every sale and it adds up to millions?"

"No," I said.

"Like that Entrapment movie, you know with that hot girl trying to get around all them lasers without getting her ass blown up?" He moved around acting out part of the scene that was playing in his head.

Santa shook his head at the Kid and then said, "Anyway, I ain't saying I got much, but if you need something, let me know."

"Thanks," I said as I returned to playing my game.

He continued leaning on my bunk as I played. After my game was over he asked, "I was wondering, did you see anything strange on your way in here?"

"Is that a joke?" I asked.

He looked at me more seriously and continued. "What I mean is, did you see any signs that seemed strange to you?"

"You mean the Dante's *Inferno* plaque they had at the top of the ramp?"

"Ah," he said, "So it is still there." He thought to himself for a minute as I dealt out another game. "It's not a good sign that the warden allows that to be up there," he noted out loud.

"I get the feeling that our hosts don't really care

about fairness and equality, or political correctness," I said.

"Really," he said with sarcasm in his voice. "I hadn't noticed."

"What I'm saying is that it's one thing to treat us like this in here, where nobody can see it, but it's another to proudly display your prejudice to the outside world."

"What are you talking about?" he asked.

"Well, when they drove us here in that sardine van and we were waiting for the garage door to open, I saw that one of the cop cars outside had a bumper sticker that said..." I looked around the room and then lowered my voice and leaned towards his ear. "It said, 'If we'd known they'd be this much trouble, we'd have picked the cotton ourselves.' "

He laughed a little and said, "You're alright College."

"How long have you been here?" I asked.

"Four months in Seminole, and now going on another six months in this hell hole," he replied.

"Ten months?" I asked.

"You get used to it," he said. "Helps that I lost most of my hearing already," he said as he pointed to the lights above us and chuckled. "Turns out all them wild party days that my mom used to discourage had a surprise benefit."

Several minutes later the twitchy man on the top bunk in front of me yelled, "Shut the fuck up!" He wildly began beating his fists on his mattress.

Santa looked at me and with raised eyebrows said, "Do you think he is talking to the lights or the voices?"

I shrugged.

After Twitchy calmed down, Santa looked at the cards I had laid out on my bunk. "Want to learn a better game?" he asked. Before I answered he reached for my cards and asked, "May I?"

He scooped up the cards, shuffled them and then began dealing them out. "This one's called Free Cell. You'll like it much better."

|||| |||| ||||

"Hey you!" yelled an officer from the catwalk. He was pointing to one of the Panamanian prisoners in our cell, the one that slept above Skeletor. "Clean up this floor." The prisoner was in the middle of a four-person game. He put his cards down and followed the officer's order. The other players waited.

After he swished the mop up and down in the bucket a few times, he wrung it out by twisting it in the yellow plastic sieve attached to the bucket. Then he mopped the room, which amounted to making sure the entire cement floor looked wet. Then he pushed the mop bucket into the day room and splashed more water around. The officer came back a few minutes later and examined his work from outside the bars.

Shortly after the officer left the catwalk Twitchy climbed down from his top bunk. He unscrewed the handle from the mop head, mumbling under his breath. Then he used his MacGyver lance to reach through the bars, across the catwalk, trying to reach the light switch on the far wall.

He struggled to hit the target, but when he eventually hit the switch the room went dark–and quiet. I could hear my head pounding and my ears ringing. The four men playing cards went in the day room where the lights were still on and the rest of us laid down.

The contrast was enormous. My whole body immediately began to relax and the sound of my own thoughts started to bubble up from the ringing. I began to sink into sleep. My shoulders relaxed as I began taking slow deep breaths. As I closed my eyes a cascade of emotionally powerful images flashed through my mind: hopes, wishes, memories, her face. I tried to focus, grabbing onto the first random image of her, watching her as we stretched in preparation for a run together. I smiled at the way her eyes glowed when she concentrated. She looked at me with that look, making it obvious that she was determined to push my limits again, making me believe that my future wasn't confined by my past.

Just as I was entering the first stage of sleep, I was startled by abrupt yelling.

"How many times do I have to tell you convicts to leave this light on? Who the fuck turned this off?" screamed an officer in the catwalk.

The officer flipped the light on and stood there with a challenging stance, glaring at us from the other side of the bars. He was proud of his polished black boots and his brand new stiff utility belt. "Ya'll need to learn some respect," he proclaimed as he busily searched the room with his eyes.

The loud buzzing was back. None of us responded to him. Then he pointed to the young white kid and said, "You. Clean the head!" The Kid got up and wiped down the toilet.

"Change out the water," he ordered. "And clean the floor."

The officer glared at him as he worked. The Kid

wrung the mop out, put it aside, then lifted the bucket up and poured its contents into the toilet. He stopped half way, flushed, and then did it again. Then he put the bucket into the shower and turned it on, waiting for it to fill up. Apparently, the officer wasn't in a hurry.

When the Kid finished swabbing the night room, he put the mop in the bucket and then used it to roll the bucket into the day room. The officer followed him down the catwalk.

Santa was sitting halfway up, awkwardly leaning against the wall and cringing in pain. "What's wrong," I asked. He didn't look up at me. "Do you need help?"

He responded in a hoarse voice with his eyes closed and his face pointed down. "No. I have back problems, and when it acts up I can't move. It just locks up. This one is mild. I'm just waiting it out." A few minutes passed before he relaxed into a normal position.

...

A couple of hours later the largest man in the room got out of his bunk and started unscrewing the mop handle again. I watched as he skillfully reached across the hall and masterfully hit the switch on his second try.

I felt anxiety, anticipating the officer's response, but I also found myself proud of this defiance, relishing the spirit of a man that would dare claim his own charge in these circumstances.

"How long are you looking at?" Santa asked me in

the dark, finally able to talk without raising his voice.

"My lawyer was talking about two or three years," I said.

"Not bad," he said, nodding his head. "Not bad."

"Please tell me that's sarcasm," I said.

"What?" he asked.

"You don't think two or three years in this hell hole is bad?"

"You won't do it all here," he said. "Things are way better in prison."

"Great," I said, "so what? I'm supposed to be looking forward to going to prison?" I imagined growing old and empty behind a razor wire fence, robbed of all passions and vigor, emotionally alone.

"Damn right," he said. "Prison is a paradise compared to this place. You get to see the sun every day, walk a track outside, eat real food, go to the gym, work out, make a life for yourself."

"Great just what I want," I exclaimed, "A prison life."

Look," he added, "at least your bit is short enough you can see light at the end of the tunnel. You'll be okay."

"What about you?" I asked. "How long are you looking at?"

"Well," he said as he shifted his weight on his bunk. "I told my lawyer to fight for a number. I can handle those numbers, it's those letters that scare me." I recalled the letters at the bottom of the chart in the Federal Sentencing Guideline, saying 'LIFE'.

Santa paused for a moment and then cheered up and said, "The Kid here is probably getting a short bit like you. Then he's going to get out there and live a straight life. Ain't that right kid?" The Kid didn't say anything.

I dozed off. Sometime later, I woke to the sound of the lights coming back on, their buzzing arriving with renewed vigor, but this time there was no violent yelling. A different officer was on shift now.

"Mail call, mail call!" the officer announced.

I quickly sat up and listened for my name.

Scarface walked to the bars and retrieved his mail. Then two others followed him. As the officer began walking away I jumped off my top bunk and hurried to the bars.

"Do you have anything there for Roberts?" I asked.

The officer continued walking away without acknowledging me. I returned to my bunk and slowly climbed back up.

"You have to let it go," Santa said.

"She's going to write me," I replied.

"Maybe," he responded, "but hanging on that cliff isn't going to do anything but make your time go by as slow as possible."

"I don't have a choice," I said. "It's the only thing I have left." Santa sensed how desperately I needed this lifeline of hope and let it be.

"Uhhhh Houston we have a problem... uhhhh, Houston we have a problem," a voice said on the loudspeaker. Apparently, a guard that fancied himself to be above average intelligence had decided to start the morning shift by entertaining himself. Laughter backed up the announcer as he continued, "Uhhhh, Houston we have a problem. Uhhhh Houston we have a problem."

Thirty minutes later, an officer came down the catwalk with a newspaper.

"Hey professor," he yelled.

I looked up at him, but stayed sitting on my bed. "Says here that you stole moon rocks from NASA."

"Does it?" I asked.

"Sure does. But we know that ain't true, because everybody knows that NASA faked them moon landings. So what'd they really get you for?" He slid the paper between the bars and dropped it on the floor. Then he continued walking down the catwalk laughing.

Santa picked up the paper and read the article.

"Moon rocks huh? And they got you sitting in here?"

After Santa finished, the Kid grabbed the paper, and gradually became more animated as he read. Suddenly he jumped out of his bunk, walked over to my bunk and enthusiastically said, "Twenty million dollars?"

"No," I said. "It wasn't twenty million dollars."

Ignoring me, he continued to read. When he finished he said, "You should totally fight this. All you have to do is take it to trial and then demand that the government bring one of them aliens from the moon, you know the ones they have in Area fifty-one, or some shit, and make it testify. They will probably throw the case out because they don't want to go public and shit 'bout the alien they been hiding, or admit that they have it. But if they do put it on the stand, you just ask it about the rocks. You know, how much they're worth and shit. It will tell you they are worthless, just fucking rocks where it comes from."

The Kid was quite proud to have put this plan together.

"Wait a fucking minute," Santa said. "So the United States government is charging you for stealing moon rocks?" He started laughing a full body laugh. "Well that's pretty fucking ironic. Where did the government get them, huh? They stole them from the moon, that's where. They didn't ask for fucking permission. They just went right up there and took them. And now they are mad at you for doing the same thing?"

After he finished laughing he grabbed the paper back from the Kid and continued reading. When he was done he stood up slowly and carefully, with one hand on his back, and tried to hand me the paper. "No thanks," I said. "Unless it says something about where my girl is in there I don't need to read it."

Still standing next to my bunk the Kid asked, "Did

you tell 'em that you was just trying to give em back?"

I looked at him, trying to read whether or not he was sarcastically jabbing at me.

"You know, that you was taking 'em so you could put them back on the moon."

"Can I see that?" the guy in the bunk below me asked reaching for the paper. Santa gave it to him. I leaned off the side of the bunk to look at him.

"You speak English?" I asked.

"So do you," my bunky replied.

"I heard you speaking Spanish earlier with some of the guys here and didn't know you spoke English too. Where are you from?"

"Panama," he said without any gusto. He was trying to read the paper. I waited until he finished.

"Is this true?" he asked.

"Is what true?" I replied.

"What they say in the paper, is it true?"

"I haven't read it," I replied.

"But you are the moon rock guy, yes? You used to work for NASA?"

"Yes," I said as I repositioned on my bunk. "I used to work for NASA."

After he finished he got out of his bunk and offered me the paper. I shook my head and said, "No thanks." Santa signaled for the paper so he gave it back to him.

"What about you?" I asked.

"I'm Hector," he said as he sat back down on his bunk.

I leaned over the bed to see his face and asked, "Do

you know all the Spanish speakers in here? Are you all from Panama?" I asked.

"We all from Panama," he replied. With discomfort in his voice, he added, "We work on same ship."

The Kid was clearly feeling ignored.

"So, are you going to do it?" he interjected.

"Do what?" I asked.

"Take it to trial," he said very seriously. "You have nothing to lose. They either drop the case or you get to see the alien they are keeping."

"I don't think it works that way," I said.

He looked offended. "What do you mean?" he asked, moving closer to me with a semi-aggressive posture.

"Well, let's just say I don't think that the government has to play fair." He was clearly unconvinced. "And even if they did, you know, have an alien," I added "there's a good chance it's not from the Moon." He still didn't seem convinced. I continued, "and there's also a good chance it doesn't speak English."

His face completely changed. "You're right. Somebody would have to teach it English first. I hadn't thought of that." He looked down at his feet for a few moments then reanimated and said, "They'd have to breed it with a human, then the baby would be half human and half alien so it would be able to speak English and Alien, and then it could teach its parent English, then it could testify."

He seemed happy with his plan.

"That might take longer than two to three years," I added.

"Yeah, but at least you'd get to see the alien."

Santa laughed and chimed in, "Maybe you'd even get to be the one to have sex with the alien."

...

"Look it's simple," Santa said. "You all are starting out at a level six." He pointed to the appropriate spot on the chart in the back cover of his Federal Sentencing Guideline book.

"If they give you an enhancement for the value, and let's just say that the paper is right and they get away with sticking it at seven to twenty million dollars."

"It wasn't that much," I said.

He gave me a serious look and said, "You need to let go of thinking like that."

"Like what?" I asked.

"Like things are supposed to be fair and shit, or that them suits are going to give a flying fuck about what really happened. Hell, the courts don't care about facts, they make up facts for a living."

"Then they shouldn't call them 'facts'," I said. All my sensitivities as a scientist were outraged.

"Well, wish in one hand and shit in the other and see which one fills up first," he said.

I paused for a moment to consider the

impracticability of this, and then asked, "How does one go about deciding which hand is the wishing hand?"

"Trial and error my boy. Trial and error," he said with a chuckle.

He directed us back to the chart. "Let's just say they give you eight levels for seven to twenty million, then you'll all be at level fourteen. Which means," he said with emphasis, suggesting he was about to reveal what was behind the curtain, "if your girl's lawyer is worth two shits, then he will push to get her a minor role departure, which gives her two levels off, putting her at level twelve. See?" He tapped his finger on the chart. "Puts her right there in zone C, which means that the judge can give her probation."

I fixated on the chart.

"All you got to do is tell your lawyer not to fight the leadership role, which will bump you up by two levels putting you at level sixteen. But your co-defendants can't get probation unless they get the minor role, so you're going to have to eat this one."

The chart had become the blueprint of my future.

Santa continued, "You want to keep her from going to prison? This is how you do it. Now remember this, your lawyer is going to tell you that his job is to argue against the leadership role by pointing out that she didn't play a minor role, that she knew what was going on just like you and all that shit. But if you want her to get probation, then you can't let that come out. Besides," he paused for a moment, straightening his back, "your lawyer works for them. Don't ever forget that."

"What do you mean?" I asked.

He turned to face me in that dramatic way preachers and bullies do when they want to give you time to think about what's coming. In a voice that suggested a schoolyard fight was about to break out he said, "He don't work for you. He works for the courts. He gets paid by the courts. The judge and the prosecutor are his peers, and he will do anything to keep a good rapport with them. His job is to play you, to make you think he is on your side, but in the end the more time you get the bigger the case looks and the more acclaim they all get for taking down the big bad criminal."

With my fingers on the chart I said, "Category one, level sixteen puts me in zone D with a range of twenty-one to twenty-seven months."

"Twenty-seven months?" the Kid said. "Shiiit, I can do that standing on my head. Still," he added, "ain't no bitch worth doing time for."

"Don't mind the Kid," Santa said looking me right in the eyes, "he doesn't know about love yet." He winked at me and then turned towards the Kid and added, "Or how much turning from it will haunt you."

"Love? Shit that ain't love," the Kid said with animated gestures. "Motherfucker had two girls at the same time," he declared, resting his case.

Santa raised his eyebrows, leaned closer to me and said, "See what I mean?" He turned towards the Kid and said, "Some day, if you're lucky, it will happen to you, you'll get all confused inside and then discover that you're more concerned about someone else's shit than you are about your own."

"That ain't love," the Kid retorted, "that's just stupid. Ain't no bitch worth doing time for."

I handed the book back to Santa and sat on the foot of his bed. "Who was she?" I asked

"Who?" he replied.

"The one that you loved," I said. "The one you still love."

He looked up as if he was recalling his colored past, and after a short pause he said, "Shit Moon Rock, my little one... she's a mother now, raising a little shit of her own, and she's good at it too." He took in a deep breath. "You know she still looks at me like she believes I can fix anything, like there's nothing in the world to be scared of as long as I'm around." He began nodding his head. "Then there's Melinda, with her crooked tooth that shows up only when she lets herself smile all the way." He laughed a little and continued, "I did everything in the world to see that tooth. Got her that ring she swore she didn't want because it was too expensive. You know, she wore it for years without ever taking it off. Told her dad to fuck off at Thanksgiving and whisked her away without even waiting for the pumpkin pie. God she made love to me that night like the sky was falling. She had a head full of amazing ideas, but she could only hear them when it was quiet. And she loved them lightning bugs, said they were the forest trying to tell us the secrets of life in

Morse code or some shit."

After another deep breath and a short pause he added, "Didn't work out of course. You know how it is sometimes. Trouble is," he paused for a moment as his eyes glowed like a child that had been completely sucked in by the smallest detail of a new marvel. Then he blinked, slightly shook his head and looked back up into nothingness. "Trouble is, that there has always been someone else, the one with no name, the one I haven't met yet. I know she's out there, waiting just like I am, trying to find me too, but now I'm going to have to miss out on being in the right place at the right time for that one to ever happen. I'll never know what she looks like, whether she likes dark chocolate secrets or rambunctious thrills. When the time comes she's going to be right where she's supposed to be and I'm going to be in a cell like this, and the moment will pass by in silence."

⳹⳹ ⳹⳹ ⳹⳹ ⳹⳹ ⳹⳹ ⳹⳹ ||

Late at night an officer approached the door, swung open the little flap of metal that covered the small window and taped a piece of paper to the glass. A few people went to the window and looked at the note. When the biggest guy in the cell saw the paper—the one with the mangiest beard that spent most of his time patting his head and twisting the spikes—he immediately started yelling and making a big show.

"Ah, hell naw. I ain't going." He rushed over to the catwalk bars and started yelling into the hallway. "You hear me? No no no. Fuck no, dis ain't right. I'm serious, I won't go." He crossed the room and banged on the metal door. "You hear me? I ain't going. I'm serious. I'm graveyard serious!" he yelled in a voice heavy with gangland notes.

I turned to Santa and asked, "What's going on?"

"Its Wednesday night," he said. "They only do transfers to Orient on Thursdays mornings."

"This is how we find out about transfers?" I asked, dizzy with confusion.

"Keeping us in the dark is how they get their kicks," Santa replied. "Most of these sick fucks like to stroke their pencil dicks as they think about how none of us know where the fuck we are, how long we will be here, how our transfers are decided, or anything that directly effects our lives." I wanted to believe that this comment was an exaggeration, but the pit in my stomach led credence to the image. "If they take a liking to you," he added in oracle tone, "they'll sign you up for diesel therapy."

"What's diesel therapy?" I asked, not sure if I really wanted to know.

"Its their special fuck you list, a one way ticket to Shit Town, where they transfer you from jail to jail, never at any one spot for more than a week, spending all your time in holding cells, shitting and pissing in a bucket, freezing to death on fucked up concrete, never anywhere long enough to become familiar with any faces, no access to a phone, not even your lawyer can keep up with where you are."

I was mortified. "Why would they do that to anyone?"

He laughed at me as if I was a naïve child and said, "Its just what happens when you give uneducated power tripping pricks a shit ton of power and no accountability. They get bored and we get diesel therapy."

After processing Santa's acceptance of this reality I continued my queries. "Why would he rather stay here than go to Orient?"

"Maybe you should ask Mr. Grave-yaud Serious," Santa replied as he wiggled his fingers in a sarcastic attempt to denote ghosts.

Graveyard Serious started kicking the door as he yelled, "Shit's 'bout to kick off up in here CO, knaw ahm talk'n 'bout? Ain't no muthafuckin' way I'm going to Orient!"

He continued banging and kicking on the door,

yelling with a slight tremble in his voice, but there was no reply from the officers. Everyone in the room was watching, waiting for a squad of combat ready officers to enter any minute, or for him to go crazy and start coming after one of us. After several minutes, he slowed down. He was breathing heavy, flaring his nostrils, with bruised fists and feet, but was still in full fight or flight mode. Then he crossed the room and starting yelling through the bars. "Ain't no transfers today. Uh uh. I ain't going!"

Over the span of several minutes he continued trying to egg the officer's on, yelling down the catwalk, slowly melting into the bars as he ran out of energy. Then with a quick look up he jerked up and swiftly marched into the day room.

"No, no, no," he yelled as he banged the telephone receiver on the payphone box. "Muthafucka dis is an emergency." Then he got quiet and stayed in the day room for over an hour. We all left him alone.

Six hours later the officers came to transfer him. He was waiting for them, leaning on the door, bent over cupping his hands around his mouth. As soon as they began unlocking the slot in our door he started pleading.

"Orient muthafuckas going to kill me man! You can't take me der. I'm asking for asylum."

"Put your hands behind your back and stick them through the slot!" the officer sternly ordered.

"I can't go, dey's gonna kill me. I'm telling you man, you gots to do something. I need to speak with my lawyer." The officer rattled his nightstick up and down inside the metal slot.

"Last time I was der one of the cops tried hitting me and my brother with one of dem sticks, so I had to fight back." He was totally breaking down and his voice was choking up. "Now dey have it out for me man. Dey gonna put me in the straight jacket and tie me to dat muthafuckin' chair, making me sit in my own piss and shit and laugh at me. You can't do this. I need to talk to your boss. Take me to your boss."

"Stick your hands out this slot now, or you're going to talk face to face with my boss!" the guard yelled as he slammed his stick against the metal door with each of his last words.

Graveyard Serious' ripped masculine stature no longer mattered. He was in tears, begging as he turned around and put his hands out the hole. "I have a right to a phone call. I need to call my lawyer," he cried in a last desperate attempt.

They cuffed him and opened the door. Two officers grabbed him at the same time and pulled him out of the cell. Then they closed the door and locked it behind them.

Twitchy climbed down from his upper bunk and moved into the lower bunk Graveyard Serious had left behind, switching out the mattresses.

HHT HHT HHT HHT HHT HHT HHT HHT I

Skeletor was alone in the day room, watching Teletubbies with utter fascination.

"Chow time, chow time, chow time" the loudspeaker announced.

Carts came rolling down the hallway and we habitually stood in line. Sugarless cornbread, grits, and a gray cardboard patty with brown salt water poured on top of it. I took a bite into the cornbread and felt something strange in my mouth. The consistency wasn't right. There was something crunchy and flaky in the middle.

I pulled it out of my mouth with my fingers to take a look and found that a cockroach had been cooked right into the bread. I had bit it completely in half. Disgusted I spit out the rest of the food in my mouth and began scraping off my tongue with my fingernails. The others started laughing at me.

"Yours was cooked in the same batch," I said. Some of them laughed harder, others began breaking their cornbread apart to look inside.

I looked at my food for a minute, half expecting something in it to start moving, then slowly began eating the rest of my unrecognizable food. Several minutes later, during a commercial break, Skeletor approached me and pointed at my cornbread cockroach. "Sure," I said, as I handed him the tray. He picked around both cockroach halves and ate every last crumb.

I leaned over to Hector, my bunky, and asked, "Why does he act like that?"

"What do you mean?" he replied.

"Why does he spend his days glued to the high pitch, annoying television as it screams out a show for babies, all the while smiling? Why does he act like he is having fun in this hellhole, or like this is the best food he has ever had? What's wrong with him?"

Hector chuckled and said, "Look at him. He's never had three meals a day in his life. He's never been in a supermarket, never seen a TV. This is the safest place he's ever been."

"You expect me to believe that?" I said.

"I'm just sayin'," Hector replied.

"I thought you said you were all being charged with cocaine transportation," I said.

"I did," he replied.

"So you expect me to believe that he's a drug dealer that's never had any money, or never seen a television?"

"Believe what you like Moon Rock, but look at him. Do you think he's ever had any money?"

Skeletor either didn't know or didn't care that we were talking about him.

"And I never said we was drug dealers. I said we all charged with cocaine transportation."

"What does that mean?"

Lowering his voice and widening his eyes, he pointed at Skeletor and said, "That man walked for nearly a month with nothing, no shoes, no money, finding food in the wild along the way, leaving his family, his village, and his shit life behind, trying to make it to docks he had never seen before, just on the hope that somebody would hire him–all because he heard a rumor that they were hiring.

When he got there, they took him on as a deck hand, on what he was told was a fishing boat. They hired me to be the cook. Can you believe it? Me, a cook, on a boat? So we set out on the water with them on their old boat, only one of us had ever been out to sea before. Hell, I never cooked for anyone but my family before. The guys, they was learning how to cast out the nets and catch the fish, but none of them was very good at it. They say they was going to teach us. They say we not need experience."

He clasped his hands together.

"Tree days out at sea, just after dark, we still no good at catching fish and a loud little ship full of men with guns come right up on us. They point their guns at us, come on our boat, make us wait and they take the captain inside the cabin. We didn't know what they was yelling about, but they keep yelling. The others was yelling at us, telling us "On you knees, stay down." We didn't know why this was happening." He paused for a moment and shook his head.

"The captain was the one that gave me the job. Good man, nice man." He looked over at Skeletor and then continued.

"Then, no more yelling—only a gun to the captain's head. They take him out with the rest of us, make him stand on side of boat so we could all see." His voice was getting louder and his words were getting choppy.

"Then they shot him right through the head," his voice struggling against the horror, "and throw him into the ocean! We was all yelling, but they was yelling louder, telling us, 'Shut up!' making us get back down and hitting us with their sticks. Two of them started running around the boat, looking for something, throwing shit everywhere, making a mess. One pulled out his knife and started cutting shit up. Then he sticks his knife into the life rings."

"The buoys?" I asked.

He nodded with tears in his eyes and continued. "He bring them to us. Open them and show us that they are full of white shit, say it cocaine. They knew we didn't know, but they didn't care. They just kept yelling at us, saying that we was in big trouble. Then we come here."

He paused for a moment, caught somewhere between his old world and his new one. Then he looked at me, and with a much quieter voice said, "The only thing that man worries about, is that his family will never know where he is, if he is dead or alive."

"When he gets to prison he'll be able to send them a letter," I assured him.

He looked at me with disappointment, squinted his eyes and cocked his head slightly. "You think a postman goes to his village? You think they have post boxes? Or numbers on their huts? You think they have phones and fancy TVs?"

Skeletor had finished eating and was back to watching his show with a smile.

After a long silence I asked, "They took you all the way here from Panama?"

He nodded.

"That's international waters," I said. "Why are they patrolling waters outside of their jurisdiction?" I asked.

"I don't know about yours diction," he replied, "I just know what they did."

I sat in dejected dismay, desperately trying to imagine how to tread water now that the surface tension of my privileged illusion had been shattered.

...

Hector and I were sitting on his bed, trying to play Free Cell with one less cell than usual. Hector tapped my leg and signaled for me to look. An officer opened the door and stepped inside. He immediately began looking around and then settled his eyes on me. Without saying a word he pointed to me and then pointed to the mop bucket.

I glared at Hector for directing my eyes into the line of fire as I slipped into my plastic sandals. Then I began the obligatory useless routine of spreading water on the floor.

The officer went back outside the cell. Just as I started mopping the officer yelled, "Move it!" A new guy stumbled in and the officer locked the door behind him. Something was off about the new guy. He had a completely shaven head, and light blue eyes that stared and shone as two faint lights at the bottom of a deep well.

He stood there for several minutes after the door was closed, clutching his bedroll. I finished swabbing the night room and then wheeled the mop bucket around the new guy on my way to the other room. He didn't move to the side. Although he was looking in a particular direction, it felt like he was looking past what was in his line of sight. I was glad he wasn't looking towards me.

I finished my task and returned the mop bucket, carefully going around him as I went through the corridor again.

"Crazy muthafucka," Teardrop said.

"Hey Moon Rock," Twitchy said, "dey brought you another Mormon to play with."

"I told you I'm not a Mormon," I replied.

"Shit, whatever you're born into you are for life," Twitchy replied.

"I think he's here to play with you Twitchy," Santa said. "Your bunky, your responsibility," Santa joked. A couple of people started laughing.

"Betta watch yo-self nigga," Teardrop said looking at Twitchy, "I don't think dis one is potty trained. Sure you want bottom bunk?" More people snickered.

"Fuck you nigga, fuck all y'all."

The newbie slowly shuffled to the bunk directly

above Twitchy, maximizing the noise he could make by dragging his feet. He put his bedroll on the bunk above Twitchy's but didn't start arranging it.

After finishing a few more games of Free Cell, and as soon as the floor was completely dry again, a few of us began working out. With my feet shoulder-width apart and a deck of cards in my hands, I lowered to the ground, placed a single card on the floor, then stood back up. Over and over I repeated this process until the deck was completely on the ground. Then I started picking them up, one by one.

The newbie didn't work out, he didn't climb onto his bed, he just focused on imaginary objects, contorting his face and randomly making sounds— honking, mimicking a dying bird, or sucking in while holding a face of delight and surprise, as if he thought he was flying off a cliff waiting the eminent splat on the rocks.

When lunch came around, the newbie was the last one in line.

"The fuck you looking at?" Scarface said in the newbie's face as he passed him to get in line. He didn't respond.

"You want this tray or not?" the officer yelled through the slot. The new guy showed his ID band through the slot, grabbed his tray and then immediately went back in the night room with it.

"I ain't having no chomo up in my shit," Scarface said. He started eating aggressively, glaring in the direction of the other room. "That nigga gots to go! I ain't shackin' up with no muthafuckin' chomo."

"That's what ahm talk'n bout," Twitchy added.

"A chomo?" I asked Santa.

"You know," he said, "a child molester."

When we finished eating we stayed in the day room. When the guards came around to collect the trays we lined up. Scarface was first. He put his tray through the slot then entered the night room with his intimidation walk, but as soon as he entered the other room he jumped back and freaked out.

"Aw fuck no! What the fuck? Muthafucka! CO, hey CO, you gots to take this muthafucka outta here."

His whole body was recoiling, using one hand to try to keep from vomiting and the other to block what he was seeing. Hector entered the room next and immediately went to the far left to get away from what he was seeing.

When I entered the room I saw the new guy wearing only his sandals and his plastic ID band squatting over his tray. A big pile of shit was covering his food. He glowered at us as if he were upset we were invading his privacy, yet simultaneously confused about why we were so grossed out.

"Muthafucka, dat nigga is cra-zy," Teardrop said.

"I ain't going near that muthafucka. He's got to go!" Scarface exclaimed.

"Trays!" the officer yelled demanding the last tray.

We heard keys and knew the officer was coming in. As soon as the officer entered the newbie started mixing his shit into his food with his hands, thoroughly

56

blending it into one smooth color. His eyes widened when looking at the officer, as if seeing a uniform meant his art was going to win first prize in the state fair. Then he wiped the slop from one of his hands on his own mouth and began blowing shit bubbles, making a show of it and baring his teeth.

"What the fuck are you doing, you sick fuck?" the officer said. The newbie looked at him, naked with widened eyes, face and hands covered in shit. Keeping his eyes locked on the officer he started to shove the concoction in his mouth, making slurping sounds as he ate.

"Holy fuck!" the officer said as he pushed the panic button on his radio.

"Aw fuck no," the kid said as he looked away. We all instinctively stepped back and covered our mouths.

"Tase his ass!" Twitchy suggested.

"Get him the fuck out of here CO. Do your job god damnit," Scarface said.

The officer was just as stunned as we were. He stood there watching as the newbie meticulously scraped each compartment of the tray and then licked his fingers. Just when it seemed he was finished he eagerly pressed his face into the tray and stretched out his tongue as if he were desperate to get the rest.

"Dat ain't right, uh uh, dat ain't right!" Teardrop said as he tried to look away.

Some of the prisoners started climbing up into their bunks to get further away. Santa had turned around and closed his eyes but the sounds were still making it difficult for him not to gag.

"Get that crazy muthafucka away from me CO!" Twitchy demanded.

When the newbie was finished the officer collected his composure and said, "You done?"

The newbie had raised his tray up to hand it to the officer, but then took it back and started licking it some more. We couldn't watch. I was trying my best not to throw up.

Several officers came to the door. Two of them came in, grabbed the naked man by the arms and pulled him out. The original officer left without saying a word.

"What. The. Fuck!" Scarface yelled as he kicked the bars in frustration and confusion.

"Probably going for the insanity plea," Santa said as he sat on his bunk.

"I'm not sure anyone could fake being that crazy," I said.

"Hell naw, that muthafucka be insane dawg," Twitchy belted.

"Don't matter," the kid said, "sick in the head or not, he ain't getting out."

"Muthafucka fucked up my zen, naw ahm talk'n bout?" Teardrop said.

"Your zen?" the kid asked with a smug little grin.

"Yeah, my zen, muthafucka, you know what ahm talk'n bout muthafucka, don't give me that."

...

Early the next morning, about an hour after the breakfast trays had been collected, the quiet man that had been patiently tearing his sheet into little strings and weaving them together since the day I arrived casually walked into the day room, just like he had every other day. No one paid much attention to it. We knew he was just sitting down, hugging his knees and rocking side to side, needing to be alone. Twenty or thirty minutes later the sheet tearer's bunky walked in the day room and started screaming. "Help! Help, Oh God Help!"

We rushed in to see what our cellmate was yelling about and found his bunky hanging with a blue face from the bars. He had patiently crafted that rope, making sure it was strong enough, testing to see when the officers were least likely to be walking through the catwalk, tied a noose high enough that he couldn't reach the ground, and committed to it. If there had been any sounds, they were drowned out by the buzzing lights. He had planned it perfectly.

"No, no," his bunky said as he tried to lift his body up by the waist. Tears were running down his face. Hector and I approached to help. At first, I looked for a way to untie the rope, but the knot was too tight. The only thing we could do was try to take the pressure off the rope by lifting him up. He was unresponsive and lifeless.

"Fuck this mutha fuckin' place," Teardrop said as he went back to his bed. Several of the men kicked and punched the metal door while others yelled down the catwalk.

"CO emergency! Hey, CO we need help!" the dead man's bunky yelled.

We stood there lifting him up, but it was obvious to us that there was no saving him. Skeletor stood in the corner. With bulging eyes and a blank expression, he fixated on the man's off-color face. We could hear officers rushing down the ramped hallway.

When the keys were at the door, the prisoners on the other side darted to the night room. Hector let go and signaled for me to follow. I let go, tapped the other man on the shoulder and said, "Come on, let's go." He ignored me. I made it to the other room just before the door opened.

Several officers entered fully charged and ready for combat, but to their disappointment their battlefield was decorated only with a man who was already dead, a man trying to lift him up, and Skeletor still dispassionately frozen in the corner like an Iguana statue.

"Get out of here," one of the officers yelled as they ushered the two men out of the room. "Go, now!" Skeletor was pushed into the night room by one of the officers.

Two officers behind shields blocked us from the room as several others discussed what to do into their squawking hand radios. After about a minute, the order to cut him down was issued over the radio.

Several officers left with the body. The ones that

stayed behind took our statements and scribbled down notes. Just before they cleared out, the officer that was in charge turned to the dead man's bunky, pointed to him and said, "We'll make sure you get credit for this."

We all sat somberly under the buzzing, flickering lights. No card games, no push-ups. We didn't have anything to say.

An hour later, a fancily dressed man, presumably the warden, came into the cell by himself as a handful of officers waited in the hallway. The dead man's co-defendant looked up prompting the warden to ask, "Are you the one that found him?"

"Yes, how is he?"

"He's dead," the warden said shortly. "But we appreciate what you tried to do. Here you go." The warden reached into his pocket and pulled out a cookie in a clear plastic wrapper and offered it to him.

The dead man's bunky looked at the cookie, but didn't lift a finger. The warden raised his eyebrows and shook the cookie, offering the inmate one last chance to accept his generous offer. The prisoner looked away with glared over eyes. The warden clearly didn't like this response.

"Have it your way," he yelled as he put the cookie back into his pocket and looked around the room proudly. He walked out of the cell with his shoulders high, boots clacking on the ground. As soon as he was in the hallway he yelled, "Shake down."

Four officers rushed in, "You heard him, shake down!" they said.

We got out of our beds and they patted us down one by one and moved us all into the day room.

They tore the night room apart, stealing most of the playing cards and the extra sheets people had stashed as others left them behind, as we stood next to the place where our fellow prisoner had found his way out.

The officers finished and left.

"No more funny business," the last officer warned as he wagged his finger at us. After the door locked we all slowly returned to our bunks.

For twenty minutes, nobody said a word. No games were played, no push-ups, just stillness. Then, in an act of gusto and anger one of the prisoners grabbed the mop handle, unscrewed it from the mop head and reached across the hallway through the bars with it to turn the lights off.

"He did the right thing," the dead man's co-defendant eventually said, mostly to himself. "He was better than me. He did the right thing." The rest of us continued to remain silent and still.

"They were going to kill our families if we talked. That's why the feds put us in here, so people would start to wonder, so they would think we was talk'n," he said, speaking to himself out loud. "We would never cooperate with these fucks! So they just made it look like we was. But he did it. People on the outs will hear about this. Now his family is safe. His family is safe. He did the right thing."

We sat in the dark, feeling the weight of the heavily

charged air. Screams from down the hall were much more audible when our lights were off. None of us were sleeping. We were just sitting or lying on our respective bunks, feeling the full weight of time's viscous flow. I wondered if the screams down the hall were from someone being raped, or beaten up, or just someone having a mental break down.

Almost ten minutes later an officer entered the catwalk. "Who did this?" The officer yelled as he banged on the bars with the handcuffs from his belt. The loud dinging sound rang in our ears. With a flip of a switch, the buzzing sound was once again piercing our ears and our faces were lit in strobe light fashion, but we weren't moved by his threat.

"I said, who the fuck did this?"

His nostrils were flaring as he scanned the room, but he got no reaction.

"If this light is ever turned off again you all are going to pay!" he threatened. As soon as the officer left the same man rose from his bed and grabbed the mop handle. Back in the dark we waited again. It didn't take long this time.

"That's it! Who the fuck did this? You're going to tell me or every last one of you is going to the hole!"

Santa's back was starting to act up, but as the old timer in the cell he may have felt responsible for us all. Or maybe, he too, was just wondering if he had the same courage as our recently escaped friend.

Speaking deliberately slow he said, "If you don't want us to turn out the lights... don't give us a fucking way to turn out the lights!"

"What did you say?" the officer said looking right at him.

Santa tried to sit up higher but his face cringed in pain. After a pause, he repeated just as slowly, "If you don't want us to turn out the lights..." His voice became more hoarse, but he pushed to finish, "don't give us a fucking way to turn out the lights!"

"Stand up and say that to my face old man."

Santa didn't move. Not because of a lack of defiance, but because he couldn't. His back was acting up. The kid spoke up for him. "He can't. It's his back. He needs help!"

Santa didn't appear to be breathing. His face was getting red.

"He needs help does he? I'll get him some fuckin' help." The officer marched off in a huff and in less than a minute he was unlocking the metal door on the other side of the room.

The kid stood between the door and Santa. "He needs a doctor. He has serious back problems. He can't stand up!"

The officer raised his stick and the kid moved out of the way. The back-up officer stood in the doorway as the irate one approached Santa and said, "I told you to stand up."

Santa didn't even look at him. The officer grabbed Santa's right hand and yanked him out of bed. Even over the buzzing of the lights we heard his back snap. Santa began screaming in a horrible way, gasping between screams. The officer hesitated for a second and then started dragging him out of the cell on his belly as he screamed. The second officer grabbed his other arm and assisted in pulling him along the floor. The door closed and the screams slowly faded until the buzzing lights drowned them out.

卌 卌 卌 卌 卌 卌 卌 卌 卌 卌 卌 ||

In the dayroom, a man wearing a fancy suit took center stage on the television, yelling with the gusto of a salesman trying to swindle *en masse* into a microphone.

"You don't have any problems. None of your problems are real. All you need is faith."

"Why is it," I said out loud to myself "that those who are incapable of empathy feel so compelled to preach?"

. . .

I had been pacing back and forth for several minutes in the day room.

The Kid entered. "Fuck. Again?" the Kid asked. I ignored him.

"Just do it already," he said with frustration.

"Its not that easy," I replied.

"Well you're not making it any easier." He approached the pay phone and picked up the receiver. "What's the number? I'll do it for you," he said.

I approached him and took the receiver out of his hand. I dialed one of only two numbers I had memorized. After a few rings she picked up.

"You can do it," the Kid mouthed as he backed away.

"Hello?" said a soft familiar voice.

I grabbed the phone with both hands and pressed it hard into my ear as my face flushed and my whole body began to shake. The electronically recorded voice took over.

"This is a collect call from a federal inmate. To accept the charges press five now. To block this caller, press seven." I heard the beep as she pressed the button.

"Hello?" Kaydee said.

Her voice resonated through me, filling my mind with scenes from another life, or was it a dream I once had? Whatever it was, it was magically familiar, memories of laughing, sneaking away from high school to kiss on the far side of that train tunnel, chasing dreams together despite the fact that we didn't have any money, camping in places we were sure nobody had ever been before, flying planes, mining for gem stones, planning for the future, making love in the observatory, gazing at the stars, her fully supporting my dream to become an astronaut...

"Hi," I said.

"I can only afford to take this one call," she said. "They charge like twenty bucks for fifteen minutes."

From the aloofness of her voice, I immediately sensed what was coming and my stomach sank.

I could hear the familiar sounds of our kitchen. She was cooking as she spoke, holding the phone between her head and her shoulder, and casually letting me know that this call didn't warrant her full attention. A male voice was in the background.

I couldn't hold back the tears. "I've really missed you," I said.

She paused for a moment and then said, "I'm sorry Thad, but I couldn't find anyone to sign you out."

"Why can't you do it?" I pleaded.

"My parents say that if I help you at all, they will disown me. I'm sorry, I just can't," she said.

"What about Eric, or Leland, or any of the professors in the physics department or the geology department?" I asked.

"I tried Thad. Everyone is afraid, you know, the Feds have been asking around and nobody wants to get into any trouble," she said.

I couldn't believe what I was hearing. "It's a signature bond! You don't have to pay anything," I asserted.

"I'm sorry Thad, but I've done all I can do."

"Did you try my friends at NASA?"

"Nobody can do it Thad," she said.

"Did you even ask them? What did they say?"

"You lied to me Thad. You told me that I was your adventure partner, that she wasn't going to be involved. Do you have any idea what it felt like to find out from the television that you did it with her instead?"

"You knew I fell in love with her," I said.

"You said you loved us both, but you said it was going to be you and me for that adventure." We both waited in silence.

"And now you can't sign me out," I said with a sigh. Frustrated, I added, "You realize that if it had been you instead, you would have been in the same situation I'm in right now, right?"

"Doesn't matter Thad, we'd still have trust," she said.

I took in a deep breath, closed my eyes, and said, "So what do you want to do now?"

"That depends," she replied.

"On what?" I asked.

"Do you still love me?" she asked.

My heart was racing as I pressed the phone to my ear tightly with sweaty hands. "Are you asking me to wait for you?" she added.

I choked up, trying to blurt out the answer I had practiced so many times, but nothing came out. I remembered Santa helping me go over it.

"Well?" she added impatiently.

A single word, all that was left of my practiced lie, barely escaped my mouth, "No."

As soon as she heard this she perked up and said, "Well then there is nothing more for us to talk about. Have fun in your new life, Thad. I wish you the best." She hung up.

I stood motionless, holding the phone to my ear, with my head slightly lowered and my eyes closed. I could hear the Kid behind me in the doorway. After waiting half a minute, he asked, "You okay?"

I hung up the phone, but continued facing it, looking through the bars, drained of all the passion that once drove me. The kid slowly left the day room, leaving me alone to regain my composure. A few minutes later he reentered the room and asked, "What was it that the old man said... about people that act surprised about lies?" I'd never seen him without his armor of sarcasm before.

I thought about it for a moment and said, "He said, 'The people to watch out for most in life are the ones that punish people for telling the truth, but then act surprised when they lie.'"

"Yeah, something like that," he said as he nodded his head, looking directly at me.

"Why do you ask?" I asked.

"No reason," he said. I tried to peer inside of him, trying to figure out if there was a hidden level of complexity surfacing from his practiced gangster veneer. "Just trying to remember," he added.

"This wasn't that kind of lie," I said.

"I know," he replied. "I know."

||||| ||||| ||||| ||||| ||||| ||||| ||||| ||||| ||||| ||||| ||||| ||||| ||||| |||||
||||| |

"Roberts," the officer yelled as he opened the slot in the door. "Lawyer visit."

I slid off my bunk, slipped into my plastic sandals, walked to the door and put my hands out the slot with my wrists together. As the officer cuffed me, I looked into the day room and felt the weight of futility in my breath.

The door let out a metallic screech as it slowly opened. I stepped outside and waited as the officer lifted the lever that closed the door. When he was finished, I followed him up the inclined hallway to a small room containing a table and four small orange plastic chairs, just slightly bigger than the kind you see in grade school. My lawyer looked at me from the other side of the table. I desperately scanned his face for signs of news. Sitting across the table from him, with their backs to me, was a professionally dressed woman in her late thirties and man in his forties with a military haircut in a grey suit.

The room was warm and quiet. The officer nodded at the suits and closed the door behind me. Brandishing my cuffs and Halloween clown costume, advertising me as guilty scum, I made my way to the open seat next to my lawyer. I sat down and rested my handcuffs in my lap beneath the table. Dead silence. I looked back and forth at each of them. The two strangers were studying me, like they had me in their scope but wanted to take their time before pulling the trigger. My lawyer was avoiding my eyes.

After ten seconds, the woman broke the silence. "Mr. Roberts," she said as she moved her hands from the edge of the table and casually interlocked her fingers, "We are with the NASA OIG, the Office of Inspector General." She quickly glanced at her companion and then continued, "We are here to ask you a few questions." I looked at my lawyer. He glanced at me and quickly looked away. The other man cleared his throat, leaned partly over the table and said, "We have some national security concerns involving several laptops that were stolen from NASA. These laptops had sensitive data on them. Can you tell us anything about those laptops?"

"No," I said with surprise in my voice.

Like she was scolding a child with chocolate smeared all over his face for claiming to not know anything about the cake, the woman said, "If you tell us where they are we will make sure they go easy on you."

"I don't know anything about any laptops," I said.

They both looked at me as if they were still waiting for my answer. My lawyer turned to me and said, "They are prepared to offer you a proffer agreement if you tell them what you know." Both suits had expressions that reminded me of the arresting officer's hostility.

"I already told you, I don't know anything about any laptops." I said. My lawyer started playing with a pen, twirling it around nervously in his hand.

The man grabbed a stack of paper from his briefcase and placed it in front of him on the table. "So," he said, clearing his voice again. "You expect us to believe that while you were stealing national treasures from NASA, you just left these laptops alone, that you have no idea where they went, or have no idea who has them now?"

I felt a sick feeling in my stomach; the kind that tries to warn you that someone is about to shove you off a cliff in the dark. Why was this happening? When was it going to end? I faded, losing track of time. They were yelling at me, not with loud voices, but with condescending voices of malice, like they were grade school bullies taunting a bug that bit them as they slowly tortured it to death, knowing that they'd never be held accountable for their actions. I couldn't make out the words. I couldn't focus. Then suddenly, I blinked and they were both sitting there silently staring at me with scrunched up brows.

"I don't know anything about any laptops," I repeated as my voice cleared another octave in mounting panic.

The woman leaned back in her chair with confidence and said, "Okay, well our offer is good for today and only today. After that, if we find out you had anything to do with it, I can promise that we will push for the maximum sentence." She folded her arms and added, "Why don't you talk it over and let us know if you remember anything."

My lawyer nodded at me and then at them. They both got up in a display of contempt. The man knocked on the door like he was rattling off a tree house entrance password with his head cocked to the side. The woman was wearing black high heels.

After they left, I turned to my lawyer and let loose. "What was that? Where have you been? Couple of days? It's been almost two months! Nothing? Not a single letter, a message, an update? You don't accept phone calls? What the fuck is going on? What's taking so long? Do you have any idea what's going on in here? You have to get me out of here!"

"Calm down Mr. Roberts," he said.

"Calm down?" My voice spiked shakily, losing hold of any remaining reserve. "Do you have any..." I shook my head trying to focus. "One guy dies, just hanging by a rope, a guard tortures Santa... snaps his back, dragging him out screaming."

He looked away, slightly rolling his eyes.

"A guy... a guy eating his own shit. There's cockroaches in my food, and the lights! The lights never stop. I... I didn't kill anybody, why am I still here?"

He let out a sigh of annoyance and then calmly said, "The wheels of justice turn very slowly Mr. Roberts."

"Justice? What are you talking about? Do you even care what happens here?"

Instead of responding, he fished out some papers from his briefcase and put them in front of me.

I twisted my body and turned my chair partially towards him and continued. "Justice? Are you listening to me? This place is a fucking shit hole. Everything about this is immoral, illegal and inhumane. Call Amnesty International. Do something! This whole place needs to be shut down."

"You really need to calm down Mr. Roberts. It doesn't do anybody any good for you to get all worked up like this. We are all doing everything we can."

"What? What are you doing? Who's doing anything?" I asked. He looked at me with distain.

I couldn't let it go. "Name one person that's doing something," I said.

"Mister Roberts," he said in a voice that reminded me of my father being mad at me for crying, after he had informed me that he had thrown my cat into the lake, in a plastic bag, with a rock to weigh it down. "You have to be patient. These things take time."

I felt the bile rising in my throat and my neck stiffen. "I don't know why you're not listening," I said under the new weight of defeat. I took in a languid deep breath and then spoke slowly. "I'm not going to survive in here. You need to get me out of here. It's your job to represent me and I'm telling you that I need to get out of here."

He tapped the papers in front of him with his pen and then held it out for me to take.

"Well to help move things along we need to have you sign this." He pointed to the signature line at the bottom of the page.

"What's this?" I asked.

"It's just a wavier," he replied.

"A wavier of what?" I asked, squinting at the page. I began blinking quickly.

"It's just waiving your right to a speedy trial."

"We're not going to trial," I said confused. "I told you to plea guilty."

"Like I told you before," he said with a patronizing slap on the wrist, "First we have to plea not guilty so we can get the Discovery. It's a normal process. Then, later we plea guilty. In the meantime, the system is really backed up, so in good faith we need you to waive your right to a speedy trial while we try to work all of this out."

I continued squinting at the paper. "I can't read this," I said. "Its my contacts. They are hard contacts, and I have nothing to clean them with, nothing to store them in at night. If I ask the officers for contact cleaner they will confiscate my contacts. Do you know I've been wrapping them in toilet paper every night, and then cleaning them in my mouth before I stick them in my eyes?"

"Its just a standard document," he said. "Nothing to get all worked up over the details about."

Leaning towards the table I continued trying to read the paper. After a minute, I sat up and looked him straight in the eyes.

"I haven't heard anything from Tiffany," I said, trying not to cry. "I don't have anyone any more. You're the only one that is on my side, the only one I have any communication with. You have to help."

"Now let me stop you right there Mister Roberts," he said rather loudly as he backed up in his chair and straightened his posture. "You need to keep one thing clear. I'm not some sort of father figure here to rescue you. I'm not your friend. I'm your lawyer. It's important that you don't get confused about that."

I felt the blood drain from my face, as his candor jilted my attachment to the world making sense.

"I'm here to do my job, and that's it," he added. "It's not personal, it's just what I do during the day. To me, you're all like a bunch of potatoes going down a conveyer belt. Once they are all bagged up, that's that." He leaned slightly forward, softened his voice and with a quick head nod repeated, "I'm here to do my job and that's it."

He stood up and turned his back to me for a moment, as if to further assert control over the conversation. Then he turned around and said, "Good, now we need to talk about the OIG proffer agreement. Do you know anything about those laptops?"

"No, I don't," I said.

"Cause if you do," he continued without any regard for my words, "now is the time to say something about it. They are willing to put it in writing that they won't add anything about the laptops to your charges if you tell them everything they need to know."

"I told you, I don't know anything about those laptops," I said. "I've never heard anything about them until today."

He tried to gauge my thoughts for a couple of seconds, then he perked up as if everything was cheery and said, "Okay, then we are all done here." He reached out, signaling for me to hand him the papers and the pen. Without hesitating I extended my cuffed hands and gave him both at the same time. He put the papers back in his briefcase and approached the door.

"I'll let you know when we are ready for our next move," he said as he looked out the little window. "Until then, sit tight and try to relax."

My eyes widened in complete disbelief.

He knocked on the door. Then, while waiting for the guard and looking out the Plexiglas he said, "You know, it's just time. Try to enjoy it." Then he turned towards me and added, "Many of us often wish that we had the spare time to just relax, that we didn't have to go to work, or pay taxes. You should make the most of this."

I clenched my teeth at his empty words, and found myself breathing harder.

The door opened. The officer escorted him away and I was left in silence. Several minutes later the officer opened the door. "Let's go," he said. I stood up and followed him into the hall. On our way down the ramp, the officer received a call on his radio.

"Go ahead," he said into the radio.

"We need Roberts up front," the radio announced. He looked at me and signaled for me to turn around. The hallways felt so spacious and open, much warmer than the cells. We approached a glass separation, like a bank teller's wall, with my lawyer on the other side.

"You forgot to sign this," he said as he pushed the papers and pen through the slot to me. The officer looked at me signaling me to take them. I grabbed them and looked at my lawyer.

"I didn't forget," I said. "I don't want to sign."

"Look," he said very agitated, "I'm not leaving here until you do."

"You can't force me to sign. I have rights," I exclaimed.

He shook his head and said, "Mister Roberts, if you want me to represent you, then you need to act in good faith." He signaled with his eyes to the papers now in my hands.

"Things will go much easier if you show some cooperation," he added.

"You heard him," the officer chimed in. I looked at the officer with surprise. He responded by scrunching the fingers of his right hand together and then air scribing. "Sign the god damn paper. I ain't got all day."

. . .

"He said what?" Teardrop asked.

"I'm not kidding," I replied. "He told me it's only time, and I should enjoy not having to work or pay taxes."

"Did you tell him you'd trade places with him?" the Kid asked.

"Dat muthafucka," Teardrop said. "You should dump that muthafucka's ass so hard, his chitlens be rubben dey's nuts for weeks."

"Welcome to the real world Moon Rock," Scarface said as he slapped me on the shoulder. "I'm telling you dawg, dey's all punk ass cocksuckers. It's fucked up, but best to be finding dis out sooner den later, know what ahm talk'n bout? Just remember it's not just the lawyers."

"What do you mean?" I asked.

"Its everyone. Every last one of dem. Every bastard on the whole god dammed planet be constantly spreading dey's own bullshit. Everybody thinks dey is the good guy fighting against a world full of villains and monsters. Dey done forgot all about trying to imagine what it's like in someone else's shoes. No no no, now it's about what's easy. And for everyone on the outs, it's a hell of a lot easier to think that all of us in here is here because we's bad mathafuckas, and dat dey is out there because dey is some kind of saints. And all of dis shit," he waived his hands around the room, "dis shit ain't nothing when it comes to what they are willing to do, how far dey's willing to go to hold onto dem lies—to feel like dey is betta den us. In a world all about spitting lies, the man with the best smelling shit is king."

Twitchy interrupted to carry on a conversation he was having with himself. "Seriously, what the fuck is up with these lights?" he said shaking his hands over his head in petulance as he shot bullets at them with his eyes.

"You know," I said, "the lights in the visit room were quiet."

"Of course dey is," Scarface belted. "What you think? We got all dis noise by accident? Shit no. Dis shit is on purpose dawg."

"I heard that it's quiet in the hole," the Kid said.

"Why don't you go and find out for us?" Teardrop asked, as if he was a sixth grader taunting a first grader trapped on the merry-go-round to just let go while continuing to spin it up faster and faster.

"Can't be worse than dis," the Kid said.

"Are y'all seeing dis?" Twitchy said. "There's a pattern in the lights, in the way dey is flashing. Look, look, der. See dat? Now watch... See, see? I think it's a code or some shit like that. Like some muthafucka be trying to organize a break out or some shit."

"Dis Muthafucka be crazy," Scarface said. Twitchy continued his glaring competition with the lights.

HHT HHT HHT HHT HHT HHT HHT HHT HHT HHT HHT HHT HHT HHT
HHT HHT HHT HHT HHT I

"That's easy," Scarface said. "A stack of benjamin's in my pocket, a big ole pile of friend chicken, some collared greens and a whole watermelon, double fisting forties, leaning back with my pants down at my feet and two white girls fighting over who can stuff my monster cock deepest down their throat."

"That's what I'm talking 'bout" Scarface's bunky said as he fist-bumped him.

"Okay, but you didn't say where," his new bunky said.

"Dat's cuz it don't matter where dawg." Scarface started laughing.

"What about you Moon Rock," the Kid asked. They all looked at me.

"We got all day Moon," Scarface said in a bit of a taunting way.

"Doesn't matter," I said softly.

"Shit, we know it don't matter, but seeing as you's the only muthafucka here dat's going to get there, might as well spit it out."

"Lost somewhere wild, maybe in Africa," I said. "Waking up in a tent next to her, watching her eyes grow full of excitement as she wakes up and wonders if today is going to be the day we are going to make that big discovery," I said.

"The question was..." Scarface interjected.

"I know what the question was," I said. "You don't have to like my answer, but it's still my answer."

"Fucking waste of all dat white privilege," Scarface continued. Could be out der fucking a whole mess of white chicks, making 'em beg for that cock, and you's talking 'bout camping with bugs and shit in the middle of Africa. Uh uh, white people is fucked up."

...

I stripped to my boxers, grabbed the almost see-through and threadbare white towel and walked to the shower. I hung the towel over the shower rod, using it as a makeshift curtain, draping it down as far as possible and carefully wrapping the corners to hold it in place at the top. It didn't hang down far enough to block the line of sight of any onlookers, whose bunks were mere feet away, but it stood as a warning to not look this way. The lack of light in the shower was the only real source of privacy.

I removed my boxers and hung them next to the towel. Naked except for my plastic sandals, I moved to the far end of the shower then pushed the button to activate the water. The focused stream of water slapped directly on the far wall, making it obvious that I wasn't really there to take a shower.

Three new cellmates had filled the empty beds. One of them was a black guy with white streaks in his hair that had been constantly trying to get anyone he could to play card games with him. Everyone had figured out that consenting to play with him meant listening to his story of how the cops arrested him again, so there were no takers. He was harmless but annoying.

There were three bunks in my line of sight. The Kid, now taking up residence in Santa's old lower bunk, had moved to the foot of his bed, with his back to the shower. Both residents of the nearest bunk were playing a card game on another bed, out of sight. The man in the bed above the Kid was trying to sleep, and the men on the furthest bunk didn't seem to be looking in my direction.

I closed my eyes and started stroking my penis, trying my best to escape to some other reality, some other time, but the details of that other world were only available in short flashes. It was almost as if the memories belonged to someone else.

The water turned off. I pushed the springy button again and continued. Faster and faster I attempted to pull away, desperately trying to focus on escaping, on connecting to the world where feelings nourish and delight.

With my eyes still closed, I started the water up again. Then I saw Tiffany's face, the look she gave me before jumping off the train bridge in her black bikini, splashing into the water, soaking up the thrill of life. With everything left in me I clung to that image of her eyes dancing in excitement as she looked at me. Those beautiful blue eyes were the only thing that was real, the only thing that mattered. Soon I was touching her soft skin with all the time in the world, absorbing the shape of her body, caressing, exploring sensations. The idea of pleasing her amplified my arousal, but it was our dream that was most exciting—how we were going to be chasing adventures together, exploring the world, making scientific discoveries that would change everything, making love everywhere we went.

I took her, pulling her body into mine, kissing her with passion. Thrusting inside her I watched the pleasure in her face—our eyes locked together.

The water turned off, interrupting my scene. I pushed the button again.

Attempting to return to that place I closed my eyes again, flexing my muscles and stroking. But this time I caught a glimpse of a different scene, one in which Kaydee was gleefully going about her life, dancing in a field of flowers with her long black hair in a light summer dress, refusing to look back at me. There was nothing to see near me, just empty darkness in the foreground, but it felt like I was tied to railroad tracks, under the hot sun, trying to escape, while in the distance she danced with blissful sarcasm, pretending that she didn't notice me at all.

I stopped stroking, looked into the cell to see if anyone was looking my way and then hit the button again. This time Tiffany was back. I was on top of her, looking down at her, at the invitation reflected in her eyes to become so much more, as her lips artfully curled into French whispers. Was it her beauty that captivated me more, or this invigorating feeling that I could be what she believed in—her James Bond, Indiana Jones, Casanova, and best friend simultaneously?

Bracing against the wall I tried to not make any sounds. The release was extremely intense, allowing me to vividly escape into that other world. I tried to hold onto it as long as I could, but it was only seconds until the darkness began to pull me back. Silent tears poured down my cheeks as the Technicolor hopes I once dared chase were suffocated by the puritanical hypocrisy of the new reality.

The water stopped again. I pushed the little metal button and closed my eyes, drowning out my tears with the sound of the tight stream of water slapping on the wall as I stayed frozen in the darkest reach of the shower.

After a few minutes, I took a long deep breath and entered the cold water. I scrubbed as much as I could and then rinsed. I had learned that the towel didn't have enough material to dry my skin, so I slid my hands from my shoulders down my arms, down my back, and legs, swiping off as much water as I could before I grabbed the threadbare scrap to finish the job. Then I slipped back into the same boxers and exited the shower.

"Did you enjoy the honeymoon suite?" the Kid asked. I ignored him.

"Lucky muthafucka," Scarface said.

"What are you talking about?" I asked.

"You's popping off to Lake County Luxury Resorts," he said.

"What?" I asked. He nodded in the direction of the door. A little note had been taped onto the Plexiglas.

"How do you know it isn't Seminole?" I asked.

"Might be, but I gots a feeling that it's Lake County." According to the rumors I'd been able to collect, we were currently in the worst place in all of Florida, so any transfer was bound to be an improvement. But then again, I didn't know how trustworthy those rumors were.

The Kid chimed in, "Its our lucky day Moon Rock." I walked over to the door and looked at the list. "Your name is Jenkins?" I said.

"What of it?" he replied.

"Nothing, it's just..."

"What?" he said, cutting me off.

"The only thing I've known you as is the Kid, that's all."

He extended his arm towards me for a handshake. "Nice to meet you Moon Rock Roberts, I'm Billy the Kid Jenkins."

...

They came for us early in the morning—maybe three or four o'clock. We were both wide-awake, sitting up, being dragged along by the current of nothingness. I had already given Hector the deck of cards that Santa had given me. The Kid had eaten his emergency stash of food—a piece of dry cornbread wrapped in a paper towel—and given away his shiny deck of cards to his new bunky.

The sound of the keys just outside our door quickened my heart, but not in the way I expected.

"Jenkins! Roberts!" the officer yelled through the food slot as soon as it was open.

I climbed down from my bunk for the last time and handed one of my blankets to Skeletor. He wouldn't get to use the blanket for long, but it didn't matter. He would receive at least a few hours of relief from his constant shivering before the shakedown occurred.

The Kid put his hands through the slot first. As the officer cuffed him I took a last look around, scanning the faces of desperation that had been my only constant for months. Only Hector and Skeletor had eyes on me. The rest were either obsessing on the futility of hollow repetition, or desperately trying to sleep despite the incessant drone of the lights.

"Roberts!" the officer yelled.

I put my hands through the slot before passing a nod to Hector followed by Skeletor. "Good luck."

As the door grated closed I kept my gaze inside, scanning back and forth between the night and day room. Just before it finished closing I took one last look at the fluorescent demons nestled in their fixtures. Then I stood there, dumbfounded by this barrier between me and mesmerizing misery.

"Let's go," the officer said as he grabbed my arm. When we reached the top of the ramp, I turned around to see if the plaque was still there. It was. The weight of its successful spell had certainly drained every last remnant of hope. The sea of tranquility forever submerged beneath the system's thick black ink.

The officer locked us in another holding cell with three other men. Two black men were supine on the concrete benches and a Mexican was on the barren floor, propped up in the corner trying to sleep. We all still had cuffs on.

"Kind of weird, isn't it?" I mused as the Kid and I lowered ourselves down. The absence of the offending buzzing lights left a sour ringing in the ears.

"Which part?" he asked, as if a single moment of what we'd shared could be considered normal.

"This whole time, all I've done is think about getting out of that cell, about escaping, going anywhere but there, and now that I'm out, away from the screaming lights, heading to God knows what, it feels... weird."

"Weird how?" he asked.

"Almost as if that cell was the only thing that was real, and the rest of my life, all of it, was just a dream. Or maybe it's that the people in there are the only ones that have any idea what reality is really like, and the rest of the world is just happily living their lives in willful ignorance."

"You just got used to it, Moon Rock," the Kid said. His tone betrayed a shared mutual anxiety for the unknown destination ahead. He turned his face to me but spoke nothing, his expression said it all: what would we have to get used to next?

We sat for a while, contemplating the temporary feel of the room.

"Do you think Pops is still in here?" the Kid asked.

"Santa? I hope not. I hope they took him to a hospital and gave him house arrest," I replied, but there was little hope in my tone.

"Shit, don't be stupid Moon. You think they gonna spend money like that? These fucktards don't play like that. Cheaper to forget about him and let him rot to death in some hole. Besides, they'd have to explain how he got all fucked up if they took him on the outs."

"They spend a shit ton of money on the air conditioning to keep it freezing in that cell," I pointed out.

"That's different," he said. "They ain't going to spend money on making things better, only worse."

"I know," I said. "He's probably still here, out-waiting them like a rock."

"Or a moon rock," he jabbed.

"Or a moon rock," I agreed. "Out there on his own."

"Hey," the Kid said piped up, eyes alight. "Do you remember the CO's face?" He contorted his visage and acted out the expression school kids used use to mock special-ed students. "What'd you say?"

In unison we said, "If you don't want us to turn out the lights, don't give us a fucking way to turn out the lights!"

We both laughed in a moment of authentic victory before drifting off into dull silence.

Several minutes later, I mulled, "Do you think our lawyers know that we are getting transferred?"

With a vacant expression, aimed at nowhere, he replied, "Ain't make no difference. They's gonna fuck us in the ass with no Vaseline. Don't matter where they bend us over to do it."

I leaned forward and supported my head in the cup of my cuffed palms, defeat once again taking up residence.

. . .

"Tucker! Roberts!" an officer yelled, startling me out of my sleep. One of the black men got up and shuffled to the door.

I took a moment to intently make eye contact with the Kid. "Guess this is goodbye. Good luck."

"Good luck to you too Moon." His rich chocolate-colored eyes were sincere.

One of the officers opened the cage door. Tucker and I stepped out. The officer relocked the cage as his companion verified our slave numbers on our plastic wristbands and crosschecked them with the list on his clipboard.

Two black men in chains were waiting despondently in the hallway, eyes down, broken of their resistance. We were directed to line up behind them and then march, which we did in the numb shuffle of chained steps. We went through two different security doors, eventually making it to the garage where a white vehicle was waiting for us. The interior cage of the van was a gaping maw, anxious to consume us.

The side door of the van was wide open. Two female prisoners were in the front bench seat, watching us approach wishing they had the ability to disappear. The tension in their faces mimicked a spiritless dog that had no further to retreat on its chain. The youngest black man in our group got in first, sliding all the way to the end of the back row. The officer directed us to follow. I was the last in line. There was no room for me in the back, so the officer directed me to sit on the front bench next to the women. Neither of them moved an inch as I occupied the seat, shoulder hunched and heads down.

One officer closed the door behind me and conversed with his radio, while the other officer attended to his clipboard.

"Hey shawty" the young black man said in a loud whisper voice as he leaned in lewdly. "Let me get some a dat pussy."

She wasn't able to turn, but her body gave no clear sign of refusal, so he took it as consent for more. He immediately began snaking his hands around the side of the bench to touch her, despite the limitation of his cuffs. The girl next to me was looking forward blankly, slumped with profound disinterest.

"Come on," he continued. "Give me yo nasty bitch, I know you want it."

She repositioned herself slightly, pushing her midsection closer to his hands. Stretching as far as he could, he managed to get his cuffed together hands down her pants. She let out sounds that were more broken whimpers than sighs of pleasure.

"Dat's it bitch. You's a nasty hoe. Dat's right, a nasty hoe."

The officers climbed into the van's front cab, separated from us by a metal cage. The two playing around tried to keep quiet as they continued, but it didn't last long.

"Hey, hey! Stop that immediately. No touching!" the officer barked.

"My bad boss, my bad," the young black man replied as he retracted back into his seat and began smelling his fingers with a Cheshire grin.

The van's engine turned over and rumbled to life as the garage door slowly opened. I couldn't see very far through the film of my dirty contacts, but I had resolved to take in everything possible about the outside nonetheless. The first moment in the glistening daylight was blinding. In desperation, I struggled to keep my eyes open and record every detail for later replay. The possibility of arming myself against the endless echoes of boredom that undoubtedly awaited me in a sunken cement cell, was more important that breathing. As we drove out under real sunlight, I was overwhelmed by how its golden rays cast depth and texture into the world. Tears began to well up in my eyes, the emotions bubbling up unbidden. It was the trees! I hid my face from the others so they could not see the tears in my eyes. A brilliant sea of glittering, dappled, radiant green surrounded us, and I... I had forgotten trees existed.

There was so much to see on the freeway that I couldn't afford to blink. I peered into every car that passed by, seeing quick glimpses into the lives of people that knew nothing about the hellhole we left, or the next we hurtled towards. I saw people marching along in a world built by apathy and blindness, using ignorance as currency. They were content with the scramble they were currently preoccupied with, blissfully wrapped in the kind of naiveté that was designed to fortify the stories in their head, the stories they had come to need. There was no tinting on our windows, yet none of those people noticed a van full of chained humans, nobody saw the cage on wheels passing right next to them.

Chapter 3: Seminole

IIII IIII IIII IIII IIII IIII IIII IIII IIII IIII IIII IIII IIII IIII
IIII IIII IIII IIII IIII IIII IIII III

Twelve of us were packed into a cement holding tank that was clearly designed by an architect with a fetish for helping depressed people become suicidal. The smell of man sweat and urine filled the stagnant air, thick and heavy. A gaunt black man in his late forties was having a loudly scattered conversation with all the voices in his head, interspersed with high pitched sucking sounds that he made with his tongue against his gold teeth.

"Oh yes you is," he blurted out, eyes wide with determined focus on the blank wall directly in front of him. His head moved in jerky muscle spasms, punctuating his statements with the tics.

"Damn you stand der like you live der," he added after another obnoxious sucking sound.

Addressing the room as a whole, rather than anyone in particular, I tentatively asked, "Have any of you been here before?" No one responded. I inquired again, louder. "In this jail I mean? What's it like in the cells?"

None of them responded to me. One of the black men was tapping his foot loudly while gazing into the ceiling. Those who had places to sit appeared to be studying the floor or attempting sleep in awkward positions. I was of no consequence and my questions fell lifelessly on them.

We were all dressed in bright red scrubs and pale brown plastic flip-flops. The cement bench was fully occupied so four of us were standing.

"Dees people ain't know what da do," Schitzo continued as he massaged his face with his palm and sucked through his teeth again, a high shrill whistle to accompany the annoying foot tapping.

"Ain't nobody stoppin' ya. Get ya' self some den," Schitzo continued to the wall. The wall didn't respond.

I sat down on the stainless steel toilet, sans its seat, and wearily rested my head in my hands with my elbows on my knees. I didn't know if I could sleep in this position, but it was worth the effort, although it wouldn't be long before someone needed the steel throne.

...

"Let's go," the guard ordered as he opened the door of the holding cell. It was just past lunch the next day, as best as I could gather with the absence of windows or clocks. Lunchtime was also completely arbitrary, only the rumble of hunger gave any indication of the passage of time. Despite our creative attempts to contort our bodies on the cement, none of us had gotten any real sleep.

We all lined up in single file, like depressed ducklings, as we exited the cell. When the last man was out, the officer yelled "Halt!" in a vaguely military tone.

The officer closed the cell door and began to cuff us. When he was finished we followed him to a junction, at which point he directed each of us, with an abrupt hand wave, to follow a different officer.

As we scuffed along the floor a few of us pulled our shirts over our noses, trying to evade the armpit-soaked air. At the next junction a blank-faced orderly, also dressed in a red outfit, handed each of us a bedroll from a laundry bin on wheels. We clutched them between our arms, and continued our shuffled march as our ankle chains clinked on the polished cement floor.

A different officer now took custody of us. "This way," the officer said as he casually led the way.

There was something very different about this officer. He was elderly, perhaps in his late sixties, and he had a kind face, somewhat reminiscent of a Norman Rockwell painting. Perhaps the most notable oddity was that he looked at each of us when he talked, almost as if he didn't believe the stories his superiors had told him about us. He was leading a pack of prisoners all by himself, unafraid and relaxed.

"Just give me a bed to die in," the inmate next to me said out loud to himself. "I don't care which bed, just take these fucking cuffs off of me and let me lay down and die."

I tried to pay attention, to memorize the path we were taking, to notice every little detail, but I found it difficult to concentrate. The glass-walled hallways revealed a hive of interconnected pods, like an ant farm for the underprivileged. Each pod housed twenty to thirty people.

"Don't matter where, CO," the inmate continued. "I'll sleep right here on the fucking concrete, just as long as I can stretch out."

"You're in here professor," the officer said looking right at me as he pointed with an outstretched arm to the pod entrance on the left. "Stevens you're over there," he added directing another inmate to the pod across the hall. We moved into our respective positions while the rest of the chain gang waited. The officer removed my cuffs first and signaled for me to wait as the sally port slowly opened. The screeching metal door was loud and lazy to open. I stepped inside the small chamber clutching my bedroll tightly to my chest. My breath shortened as the door closed behind me with a sharp clang, tapping me in this tiny space. Then the door in front of me began to slowly open.

As I stepped inside my new universe, I felt the lack of vibration right away. I closed my eyes and took a long deep, grateful breath.

The lights were quiet.

The entire left wall of the pod was glass, inviting voyeuristic officers to satiate their needs. Cells with blue metal doors lined the wall directly in front of me and the wall to the right. The common room was decorated with four stainless steel tables that were bolted down, all currently being used for games. Two were hosting four-player card games and the other two were hosting some caveman version of Dominos, played by standing around the table, slamming a Domino down as loud as possible when it was your turn, vibrating all the pieces already on the table, and then pounding your chest and verbally taunting the other players until it was your turn again.

There were two levels, connected by a blue metal staircase right next to the glass wall. Upstairs to the far right, a young dark-skinned man with a shaved head was beating on the railing while rapping, restarting the same tune every time he made a mistake—over and over again. All but one of the metal cell doors were wide open. A large public shower was adjacent to the sally port I had just gone through.

A man with a pale face and a bald spot that spanned the entire girth of this head was sitting on the stairs, mouth breathing and gawking at me. The hair on the sides of his head was raked towards the center, unevenly twisted together in the middle to keep it in place, making it officially the worst comb-over I had ever seen. Without breaking his piercing gaze, Comb-over slowly stood up and approached me with a shoulder-heavy swagger, a roll of stomach fat hanging below his shirt.

He stopped a mere foot away from running into my armful of supplies, then began looking at me from different angles.

"You don't look like a criminal," he said. Many of his teeth were dark and his breath smelled like an animal that had been dead for weeks.

"Thank you?" I replied apprehensively.

"Do I know you?" he asked. "You look familiar."

"This place is huge," I replied, changing the subject and taking in the new surroundings. "Do we always get to be in this space?"

"No, they lock us down at night, and for counts," he said. He was still moving around me, contorting his eyebrows into funny shapes. I couldn't tell if it was simply in my general direction or a response to my face.

"Or whenever else they feel like it," he added, finally coming fully upright.

He put his hand on his chin and suggestively accused, "I think I've met you before."

"I don't think so," I said.

I scanned the cells, making mental notes of the density of inhabitants. There were eight of them on each floor and they all appeared to be full.

"Dat's the guy from T.V." declared a tall black man who was standing around one of the tables, but not playing the game. He approached me, cocking his head to the side with a squint. "You dat Moon Rock guy aren't you?"

"That's it, I knew I recognized you from somewhere," Comb-over said as he snapped his index finger into his middle one in triumph.

"Shit man, that's some dope shit," another man said. "You was plastered all over the motherfuckin' news man."

"Did you get to keep the money?" Comb-over asked. His breath was inescapable and gag-worthy.

I let out a blasé sigh, wishing the world was interested in real conversations.

"I heard dey was werf a hundred million," one of the black man playing cards at a table said. Several others in the room were watching us now.

"No," I said, "they weren't worth a hundred million." They were watching me with palpable interest, slowly circling in. "Do any of you know which cell I'm supposed to be in?" I asked.

"Millions?" Squinty said. "Shit, moon rocks be least billions nigga. You know how far away da moon is? Shit, that shit be muthafuckin' priceless."

"But you stashed some of it right?" Comb-over said, "Or kept some of the rocks?

" 'Sides," Squinty continued, "moon rocks is magic, gots all kinds of powers. That's why they glow and shit."

"I always wanted a moon rock," Comb-over said.

I sighed and resolutely continued through them in search for my spot.

"Fuckin' moon rocks," Squinty continued with a tone of authority. "Damn straight, dat some serious shit."

"There's only one open bunk," Comb-over said as he followed me. He pointed to a cell near the middle of the long wall on the bottom floor—the only closed door in the pod. I approached and slowly pulled on the looped metal handle.

It was dark inside the cell. The only window was a cut out in the door itself. Just inside the cell was a light switch. In the far left corner there was a stainless steel toilet-sink, the spork of the bathroom appliance world, with a polished rectangle of metal pretending to be a mirror bolted to the cinderblock wall above it. A rusty steel bunk bed occupied the right. My new bunky was curled up on the bottom bunk, knees to his chest and his blanket up to his neck. As I walked in, he pulled the blanket over his head. The top bunk was unoccupied, sporting a green plastic mattress two inches thick, but no pillow.

I arranged my linens on my new bed as my new bunky tossed and turned in the rack below, moaning like he was sick, but never acknowledging me. Comb-over stayed outside my cell.

After I finished, I went back out into the common area.

"Close the door!" my bunky yelled. I closed it as much as I could without forcing it to latch.

Comb-over was still standing there, waiting for me.

"Is my bunky sick?" I asked.

"He's just coming down," he replied.

"With a flu, or a cold?" I asked.

"No, coming down." He over-emphasized the down. "You know detoxing, riding the tail of the dragon, coffin surfing."

"Oh," I said, feigning understanding. "Okay, well what about the lights?" I asked.

"What about them?" Comb-over replied.

"Do we get to turn them off whenever we want?" I asked.

"In your cell yes, but these lights," he pointed overhead, "are controlled from out there." He pointed outside the glass wall. "They turn them off at night except during count."

"And the pillows?" I asked, expecting a nonsensical answer about another random rule.

"What about them?" Comb-over responded.

"Well my bunky has a pillow," I said hesitantly.

"You don't?" he asked. I raised my eyebrows.

"Well someone prolly snatched it up before you got here. Supposed to have one pillow to every bed, but some of dees fucks want to be special and stuff two pillows inside of one."

A light skinned black man with Rasta dreadlocks down to his hips came rushing down the stairs.

"Ahhh shit," he said animatedly, hands near his dreadlocks. "Hey hey, check it dawg, I been following your case since the beginning." He emphasized his words with a rapid wood chopping motion, head angled hard to the side. There seemed to be a connection between the aggression of his gesticulations and a desire for me to respect him immediately. "Dat's some fucked up shit dey's trying to pull on you my nigga."

"Did you just call me your nigger?" I asked in careful monotone.

His posture completely morphed, his face settling into a serious mask. Standing as tall as he could he leaned in authoritatively, "Its nigg-a, with an 'ahhh', not niggerrrrrr. Dat's for racist people." He hit me lightly on the shoulder, straightened and continued with his previous enthusiasm.

I nodded, logging this critical difference alongside 'flammable' and 'inflammable'.

"So check it... how did you get that safe out of there?" His eyes were wide bright and curious, brows furrowed slightly.

"Cause Howard Stern be like, 'Shit, if he is smart enough to break into NASA and get out of there with a whole safe full of moon rocks, then NASA should thank him for showing them the weakness in their security and hire him to be their new security specialist.'"

"You heard about my case from Howard Stern?" I asked in complete disbelief.

"Fuck, the Late Show with Jay Leno, the Late Late Show, on every news channel... everywhere."

"What about Oprah?" Comb-over asked with a chuckle.

"Shit nigga, just cause I'm black don't mean I watch Oprah!" Rasta exclaimed. Then he faced me again and continued with even more determined curiosity. "Howard Stern been talking about you for months now. And my nigga Leno says you was smoking them rocks. What's that like?"

A doughy, plump-faced white man listening to our conversation with crossed arms interjected, "Motherfucker, I heard about this shit in my truck, just before I got arrested." He had the look of a farmer, minus the coveralls and a long weed sticking out of his mouth. "Howard Stern is like your fan, man! You should call him and get him to get your ass out of jail, start some kind of public campaign or some shit."

"Fuck the world, fuck the world," the rapper upstairs sang for the thousandth time as he pounded on the railing.

"Dat's right, dat's right," a black man yelled as he slammed his Domino down on the table and proceeded to puff his chest out. "Ya'll mutha fuckas ain't shit. What you gonna do, huh? What?"

Just then, a tall and muscular black man exited his cell and ventured down the stairs with the gait of a leopard. The Farmer looked away. Both Rasta and Comb-over stopped talking until he passed.

The muscular man passed by slowly, with his towel thrown over his shoulder, with a pleased and confident air.

"Who's that?" I asked as I took stock of their reactions.

"That's Preacher," Rasta replied. "You don't want to get in his way."

My eyes followed Preacher as he moved towards the shower. Comb-over stepped into my view and, without making a sound, shook his head ardently.

"What?" I asked, not quite understanding the gravity of his statement.

"Ain't worth it man," he whispered solemnly.

Sounds of water started echoing throughout the pod.

One of the tables cleared up and Rasta signaled with his head for me to follow him, claiming the table before anyone else could.

"You play chess?" he asked.

"Not for years," I replied suprised—both for having misjudged him for someone that wouldn't have pursued such a game, and there being access to a chess set in this forsaken place.

"I've been looking for some competition," he said. I situated myself at the table as he energetically ran behind the stairs. He returned with a boxed-up chess set grinning from ear to ear. Comb-over sat at the table with us and folded his arms, watching as the board was set.

After several turns traded, the shower went silent. I couldn't help by watch as Preacher padded out in his plastic sandals and his white boxers, which, like all the rest of our issued boxers, had an opening front and center that didn't button closed. He was holding his neatly folded issued outfit, referred to as Reds, in one hand, and a small bar of soap and towel in the other. He was completely void of body fat, just a tower of raw muscle and a few scars for texture. He slowly stalked up the stairs and returned to his cell, like a big cat returning to its den.

・・・

In the middle of our third game, a young male officer opened the food slot in the glass wall and yelled,

"Mail call, mail call, mail call!" His voice cracked a bit on the third chant.

He called out three sur names at a time, along with the last three numbers from each of their 'the government owns you now' numbers, and then waited for all three to approach and collect their mail. He checked each inmate's wristband before passing the letter to him, then he moved on to the next batch of three.

"Cartwrite, oh one eight, Hanaway, oh two one, Barnes oh one seven" the officer yelled. My bunky came clambering out of our cell to get his mail. He stretched his face as he approached, then pressed his wristband against the glass. The officer pushed a small package through the slot. As he turned away, my bunky tucked the package under his shirt, went directly back into the cell, and closed the door as far as he could without latching it. I continued listening as each name was called, intently watching as each letter got passed out.

"It usually takes a week or two for the address changes to go through," Rasta said. "You'll get your letter then." The officer closed and locked the slot. "Your move," Rasta said. We resumed playing and the officer moved to the cell across the hall for their mail call.

"So, what was she like?" Comb-over asked.

"Who?"

Rasta cut in, "What you mean who? Your shortie, the one you stole them moon rocks for?"

"How do you know she wasn't taller than me?" I asked, fighting his use of words.

"What?" he asked, completely confused.

"Never mind," I said, giving up on making that point. I tried to keep my mind focused on the board, contemplating my next move.

Comb-over didn't want to let it go, "Cuz I seen the mug shots of you two, looked like you just did some college prank and didn't expect to get tossed into this fine gov'ment housing for it."

I still didn't say anything, not wanting to give him access to details about her.

"Must have had a super tight pussy for you to have done that," he added.

"Dat's what I'm talking about," Rasta said as he raised his fist towards Comb-over. They knocked fists together as if they were congratulating themselves for making some kind of profound discovery.

I made my next move and looked at Comb-over sternly.

"What?" he said. "Just sayin'."

"Ain't nothin' to be shamed of," Rasta said as he became even more animated, jerking his hands back and forth. "Shit, if the pussy tight 'nough, I'd steal me a whole planet to keep dat where I can tap it every day and every night." They both started laughing. I pretended to ignore them, appalled by the way their lack of emotional depth emptied romance of its entire allure.

"You still together?" Comb-over asked.

"Pffff, course they still together nigga, you think he look'n at that mail slot like that 'cause he wait'n on a letter from his priest?" Rasta said.

I struggled to keep my face from advertising my fleeting bit of strangled hope.

Comb-over seemed satisfied with Rasta's response. We all looked at the chessboard for a bit and then he said, "My grandma used to watch some black and white movie, or some shit, where this guy wanted this girl so he lassoed the moon for her. Is that where you got the idea?" I remained unresponsive, unwilling to allow them to trample on any of the actual details of that beautiful intimacy.

Several minutes later, the officer began flickering the lights off and on. "Lock down!" he yelled. I started to get up.

"Hurry," Rasta said, "Make your move."

"Let's just leave it here and finish afterwards," I said.

"It will be chow time afterwards," he said.

People were slowly moving towards their cells, pulling their own doors closed until they locked with a loud metallic click. We started playing quickly.

"Got you," Rasta said. "Check."

"You win," I said.

"Not yet," he said.

"It will be check mate in three moves," I said. "Let's go." He looked around with his nose high and raised his hands as if he were waiting for an imaginary crowd to recognize his great achievement.

We cleared the board, putting it back in its box and went into our separate cells.

I pulled the door closed behind me until I heard the click.

My bunky was hunched over his new mail—a hardbound book shipped from Barns and Noble. Clearly he wasn't very interested in reading it. He had torn the cover off and was scratching at it with a small razor blade, carefully collecting the resultant pile of powder on the page below.

"Nice to meet you," I said a bit unnerved.

He looked at me with a touch of paranoia. "You want some, don't you?" he asked.

"Some what?" I replied.

"Don't play stupid. Dope." Then he turned his head towards me and said, "But not just any dope, this be the finest dope in the hood." I didn't want to tell him that I still didn't know what he was talking about. I had heard several people talking about their different drug experiences and as far as I could tell "dope" was a catchall name for whatever drug you used most regularly.

"My boy took care of me," he added. "Damn straight," he said more to himself than to me. "And now that you're my bunky, guess my lucky day means your lucky day."

"That's just a book," I said.

"A special book," he said. Still scraping away he turned his head towards me and smiled proudly. "This here, be the good book," he said, adding emphasis on the 'good'.

"Where did you get that blade?" I asked.

"What's with the twenty questions, huh? Are you a fucking narc?"

"Just new," I said. His posture changed, almost as if he completely forgot about his task at hand.

"You look like an undercover cop," he said. He began to look at me more intensely, searching my lightly incredulous face. "Where did you just come from?" he asked, pinching the razor blade between his fingers and slightly waving it around with his words.

"What do you mean?" I asked.

"Before here, before Seminole, where were you?" he asked.

"The Submarine," I said. He leaned towards me with suspicion. I added, "You know, Morgan Street."

"How many stairs do you have to go up to get to the cells in Morgan Street?" he asked with a baiting tone.

"None, you go down a long ramp, at least where I was," I said.

"Okay, you're cool," he said dismissively. He turned back to his project and continued talking to me without looking at me.

"When they hand out razors you can carefully pop open the new one and pull out the blade. Takes some practice, but you'll get the hang of it. You just put the dull one back and presto, new blade."

"How do you get the first one?" I asked.

"Gum wrapper," he replied right away.

"Gum wrapper?" I asked, completely confused.

He let out a sigh of contempt and leveled his gaze at me. "You take a gum wrapper and fold it to just the right size then you put it in place of the blade and then snap it back together. When you take the razor back you show it to the CO and then drop it in the trash. Works every time."

"Okay, but where do you get the gum?"

"You don't get gum, just the wrappers," he said.

I stood there with a blank expression, wondering how he thought this made sense.

"Jesus!" he exclaimed. "You get one of the orderlies to snag wrappers from the officer's trash. You sure you ain't a narc?"

Instead of responding I drug my gaze across the floor, up to my bunk, and dispassionately ascended.

After scraping away for several more minutes, he carefully tore out the page his tailings were collected on and then scraped it all onto the exterior glossy side of the back cover of the book. Then he used the razor blade to arrange the powder into little lines—tapping and separating. When he was satisfied he took the page he had torn out of the book, tore off a strip and rolled it into a straw.

"You sure?" he asked.

"I'm sure," I said firmly. "I only need sleep."

"More for me," he said cheerily. He snorted all three lines, punctuated with a thick sniff, then shook his head from side to side and casually laid down on his bunk.

...

I woke abruptly to the loud clank of the cell door popping open.

"Chow! Chow! Chow!" yelled the officer through the same slot in the glass that the mail had been passed through.

I climbed down from my bunk and vacated the room.

"Close the door!" my bunky yelled even though he was already climbing out of bed.

When I made it to the front of the line, an orderly on the other side of the glass slid a tray of food to me through the opening.

There were only sixteen seats available on the tables. All of them were taken by the time I got my tray. Some inmates returned to their cells to eat dinner alone, others made room on the floor in the common room. I sat at the bottom of the stairs and looked at my food.

"Let me get your roll," Rasta said as he went around me on the stairs and sat a few stairs above me.

"Hell no! Let me get yours," I replied. I didn't know what any of the rest of the food in my tray was, slop differentiated only by their color, but I recognized the roll. I saved it for last, a reward for consuming the barely edible puddles. The roll was cold, individually wrapped in plastic, and felt hard in my hand. After removing the plastic, I tore a little piece of it and placed it in my mouth, closing my eyes, attempting to absorb every molecule of it. My neurons lit up, sparking a lightning storm of sensation memories, nuanced pleasures kept alive in silent echoes. The smell of rising bread in the oven, cold winters warmed by unbridled anticipation as I rubbed my hands together and salivated in sync with the timer.

"Miss Chaterdee used to make the best sweatbread," Rasta said.

I opened my eyes and asked, "Who is Miss Chaterdee?"

"She used to run the kitchen at the orphanage," he replied. "It would melt in your mouth like butter, mmmmm mmmmm, hot... could smell that shit a hundred yards away." His eyes were now closed, conjuring the memory.

"Some day I'm going to have some real mashed potatoes again," I said. "With a T-bone steak, stuffing, creamed beans, and strawberry shortcake."

"Naw, gots to go foe some fried chicken and a nice cold beer," Rasta said.

"Beer?" I asked. "Your taste buds are broken," I said.

He laughed. "I bet you's looking forward to some warm grits and eggs in the morning."

"Are you serious?" I asked.

"Well minus the eggs," he replied.

"Ewww gross," I said.

"Cool. Then I call dibs," he said.

...

After chow was over, they didn't lock us back in our cells, so I started roaming around this spacious universe. I slowly walked up the stairs, looking behind myself every few seconds. I couldn't escape the feeling that I was going to get into trouble for being out of bounds. But I heard nothing from the cops and my fellow inmates seemed completely unconcerned about my climb up the stairs. As I approached the top, I noticed that the first cell was decorated to give off a vibe of being little Mexico. Outside there were several towel-chickens masterfully hanging from the bars as if it was a market.

"How did you do this?" I asked the man leaning in the doorway with his arms folded.

"Do what?" he asked. His beard was very intricately patterned, perfectly groomed and neat.

"Make those chickens?" I said gesturing to the terry cloth fowl.

He smiled and pulled one of them down, then carried it inside his cell and signaled for me to follow. He unrolled it on his bed and showed me that it was just a regular issued towel. Then he rolled opposing ends up into little tubes until they met in the middle and glanced up to see if I was following. I nodded, curoius. Then he reached inside each roll, pulled out the middle, pinched the protruding tabs together and then flipped the entire thing over. Next he swapped the ends that were held together, putting the ends of each tube with the end that protruded from the other side and then pulled the two groups apart. The result spectacularly resembled a featherless chicken.

He saw I was pleased and hung the chicken back in his marketplace window.

Inside the cell, an artist was cutting hair masterfully. Another was using M&M's to color a design that decorated the exterior of an envelope. The toilet was adorned with a handcrafted square cover, weaved together from folded newspapers.

"You need a cut?" one of the guys in the room asked. "Three stamps," he said.

"No thanks," I said. "Just looking."

The precision of his work was amazing. The fade was as good as any machine cut I had ever seen. I turned back to the finely groomed chicken craftsman and asked, "How is he doing that?"

"Hey Chico," he said to the artist. With a nod he signaled for him to pass his instrument. He handed it to me. It was one of the black combs we had all been issued with a razor blade fixed to it. Two teeth of the comb were bent back slightly, making perfect fits for the holes in the razor blade, which was slightly angled to give control over the cut length based on what part of the comb was used. It was a tool of genius. I handed it back to him and watched as he expertly combed through another Mexican man's fine hair, resulting in a perfect fade. Mr. Neat seemed pleased with my appreciation of this ingenuity.

I excused myself and continued exploring.

In the next cell, two men were playing cards on the bottom bunk whilst another was sleeping on the top bunk. I turned right and noticed that the first cell on this wall was a one-man cell, occupied by Preacher. He was doing triceps push-ups off the side of his bed. I kept walking in exploration. The next four cells were two-man rooms and they all had toilet covers, with different newspaper woven patterns. The last cell was also a one-man cell. Someone was sleeping in there, door wide open.

As I started to walk back towards the stairs, I heard a hissing sound coming from the cell that was directly above mine on the floor below.

"Tssss, tssssss" It was clearly directed at me.

"Ey, ey" the voice continued. A tan man in his later fifties was sitting on his lower bunk, jerking his head at me, signaling for me to come into his cell. He was bald on top, with shaggy salt-and-pepper grey hair on the sides. His hands were leathery and tough. His bunky, a young and thin man with a black goatee, was on the upper bunk leaning with his back against the wall, looking at me with harmless regard. I stepped inside the room.

"You that NASA guy, right?" the older man in the lower bunk asked.

I glanced back up at his bunky, who shrugged at me and shook his head slightly.

"Yeah," I said with a bit of hesitation.

"That mean you can read?" he asked.

The younger man on the top bunk looked at me with a smile, clearly holding himself back from laughing, stifling any sound at all.

"Yes, I can read," I replied, in wait of the punch line.

He pulled out a letter from under his mattress and held it out to me as he inquired, "Can you read this?"

I took the letter and looked at the envelope.

"Very pretty handwriting," I said. "Who is Julie?"

"That's my wife," he replied with a hint of impatience. She's in the Windy City. That's where I'm from. All my life."

"Windy City?" I asked.

"You know, Chi Town, Chicago," he said.

"Why do you want me to read a letter from your wife?" I asked.

He scooted over on his bed, making room for me to sit. "I want you to read it to me NASA. I never did let them squiggles reprogram my brain. It's just the man trying to get you down."

"What is? Reading?" I asked.

"You bet your ass. That's how they get up all in your mind," he said as he pointed to his head. "Make you think however they want. But they ain't getting me. I know their game, I can see exactly what they are up to." He signaled more sternly for me to sit next to him. I sat down and opened the letter.

"My Dearest Love," I began.

118

"Yeah, yeah," he said waving his hands. "See what the bitch wants."

"Margaret's school play was a hit. She looked absolutely adorable in that little blue dress." He was quiet and unresponsive as I continued to read Julie's description of the play and how nervous Margaret was to participate until someone complimented her performance, sparking a well of excitement in her. Then, after relaying a report on how the week went for the two of them, I turned the page over and continued.

"Yesterday we took her to the dentist and had to get her braces. It was quite expensive so there's not much left over to send you this month, but I have put one hundred and fifty dollars in your commissary for now. If I can get more to you later I will. We both miss you so much. When can we come see you? Have you heard anything new from your lawyer? I called him three times this week and left a message every time. He still hasn't gotten back to me. Please let me know if you have heard anything. We pray every night to have you home with us soon. Love Always, Julie."

"Shit man," he said in frustration. "A buck fifty? What am I going to do with a buck fifty? That bitch better send me my money." He got off his bunk and lifted up the top part of his mattress where he had some supplies stashed. Then he handed me a piece of paper and a short pencil. "Write this for me NASA. Now look here bitch, just because I'm in here, don't mean you gonna stop showing me my respect. That my money, not yours, it's three hundred a month, not a buck fifty, not two." He looked at me, "well, are you going to write or not?"

I started writing... "Dear Julie, thank you for your thoughtful letter and for your warm love. You have both been on my mind constantly. Don't worry about the money, I will be just fine with what you've already sent. If you find a way to scrape together the rest then please get yourself and Margaret something nice, or go out to a nice place for dinner."

"Then tell that bitch that my little girl don't need no braces. People ain't supposed to have straight teeth and shit, it ain't natural and don't look right anyway."

I finished with, "I'll let you know when I find out anything from my lawyer. Until then, just relax and keep living your life. Thank you for being there for Margaret when I can't."

"How do you want to sign it?" I asked.

"You sign it," he said.

"No, I mean, what name should I put?"

"She knows who it is," he replied. I ended it with "Love Always."

· · ·

"Chow, chow, chow!" yelled the officer as he electronically popped the doors open. Everyone stumbled awake and rushed out to get in line for breakfast. By the time I got my food, Rasta was already sitting on the stairs with his tray. I sat below him and he immediately leaned over and started attempting to scoop up my grits. I pulled my tray away.

"What the fuck dog?" he said. "We had a deal."

"What deal?" I asked.

"You said I could have your grits every morning," he said, like he was offended.

"I never said anything like that. And even if I had, exactly how is that a deal? What am I getting out of this arrangement?"

"You said you didn't like grits," he replied.

"Of course I don't like grits. What's there to like? Then again, I've been starving to death for months now and can't afford to give away one single calorie."

A young black man that had been the last in line approached us with his tray. The left half of his hair sported a tight intricate weave and the right half was sticking straight off his head intentionally frizzed and puffed out. His comb was in his hair like an ornament.

"Nigga, don't you know ya history?" he asked, cutting into our conversation. He was looking directly at Rasta and ignoring me. Then he suddenly switched his gaze to me and asked, "When da last time you ate grits, NASA?"

"What?" I asked.

"On the outs, before you went down, how often did you eat this?" he asked.

"I had never heard of grits before I got arrested," I said. "I don't think it's real food," I added. "In fact, I'm willing to bet that where I come from you'd get child abuse charges if you tried to feed this shit to your kid on a regular basis, due to the whole zero nutritional value factor and all."

"That's what I'm talkin' bout," Rasta said. "Dis my people's food so give it here."

"Dis ain't yo people's food," Frizz sternly said as he looked at Rasta. "Dis just another example of the man trying to keep us down. Dey want us eating this shit to remind us."

"Remind us of what?" Rasta asked.

"That we is never gonna be nothing but slaves to them."

"Pffff shiiiit," Rasta replied.

"Have you ever grown corn?" Frizz asked.

"What like, with one of them scare crows and shit, and dem long fields where some fuck with a knife for a hand be waiting all day to get someone?" Rasta was clearly pleased with his own words.

"Muthafucka, you know what I'm talking 'bout," Frizz said.

"No, I ain't ever grown any fuckin' corn. Do I look like a farmer to you?" Rasta replied impudently.

"Well if you did you'd know dat der's different kinds of corn," he said. "Der's the good shit, the shit the USDA or some shit puts der muthafuckin' stamp on, declaring it fit fer human consumption, den der's the stuff dat ain't good enough for humans to eat, da kind cows and goats be munching on and shit. And den der's the shit dat even the cows and goats won't touch, which goes to the muthafuckin' chickens." He pointed to the grits in Rasta's tray.

"Muthafuckin' chicken feed, dat's what dis shit is," he continued. "Crackers used ta throw dis shit on the ground and make dey's slaves get down on der hands and knees and eat it off the muthafuckin' dirt, pecking at the ground like fuckin' chickens so they could impress dey's cracker friends 'bout how der slaves will do anything. Dat's what this shit is. And now dat dees crackers gots der new slavery, locking us all up here, making der money off of us, dey feed us dis shit to remind us what we are to dem."

"What about this muthafucka? Rasta asked. "If this is the new slavery for all us niggas, how come they got my man, Moon Rock, up in this shit hole eating the same shit, huh?"

Frizz didn't miss a beat. "Moon Rock be an accident dawg. Dey set up the system to snatch all us niggas up. He just collateral damage so dey don't have to tell demselves the truth about the situation. White people like to tell demselves they ain't racist as they smack down dat gavel, it makes 'em feel good." He leaned in towards me and added in a quieter, conspiratorial voice, "You tell em you's a Jew or a Muslim and dey won't make you eat this shit no more. Give you special food, damn straight."

"So, then, Rasta said, "if you'd like to take a stand against all this slavery and shit, I'd be more than happy to take that slave food off your hands." He extended his tray making it easy for Frizz to transfer his grits onto it.

"Fuck naw nigga," he replied. "I don't want to eat this shit!" he said. "But I ain't got no choice. I got's to keep my strength, so I can throw down when things pop off. But dat don't mean I can't see through dey's game. Gots to stay smart!" He walked away proudly and found his own spot to eat.

Rasta was wide-eyed waiting for me.

"What?" I asked. His eyes looked down at my tray. I just started eating my gruel. Rasta ate too.

"You know... Dat shit about the chickens ain't true, right?" he said with a mouth full of food.

"Isn't it?" I replied.

"Nope," he said confidently. "I seen chickens before. Some of dem muthafuckas are fat shits. No way dey's eating this shit. I'm losing a pound a day on this."

. . .

"Trays," the officer yelled. We all lined up to pass our trays through the narrow slot. An orderly on the other side of the glass collected and stacked them on a cart while the officer watched.

Rasta and I sat down at one of the empty, dull metal tables. He already had the chess set in hand.

"Order forms!" the officer yelled after the last tray was accounted for. Rasta went to collect a form and I continued setting up a chess game.

"Got you one Moon Rock," Rasta said as he returned. He placed it on the table in front of me. I looked over the commissary order form.

"When do they…" I began to ask.

Rasta cut me off. "They take 'em at dinner," he said. "Then sometime tomorrow they bring the shit, or at least whatever they ain't out of. Fuckers never have my Pork Rinds."

Windy City's young bunky approached and sat at our table.

"You some kind of Arab?" Rasta asked him as he was contemplating his first move. He didn't reply.

"You know, like a towel heads or some shit?" Rasta added.

"I'm Indian," he replied.

"Feathers or dots?" Rasta asked.

"From India," he replied. "My name is Martin."

Rasta looked back and forth at me and Martin, like he was still waiting for his answer.

"Dots," Martin said irritated at his vast ignorance.

"Ain't no thing," Rasta said. "As long as you is a Christian, don't matter where you from." Now Martin started to look uncomfortable, but it wasn't clear if Rasta noticed.

"Want to play the winner 'Martin from the Land of Dots?' " Rasta asked.

"Sure," he said. As the game unfolded Martin leaned towards me and said, "What you wrote in the letter… that was kind."

"Thanks," I said, "but I'm kind of regretting it already."

"Why do you say that?" he asked.

"Because now she's going to get that letter and think that her husband is all of a sudden supportive, and caring, and decent, and she's going to put even more energy into being there for him. Would have been better to just let her know what he was really saying and hopefully she'd find something better."

"Better for her maybe, but what about for him?" Martin asked.

"Also better for him," I said.

"I don't know," he replied. "I think she's the best thing he's got."

"I don't doubt that," I said. "I'm just saying that if there's any good in him, then one day, when he's completely done destroying her, he's going to realize the damage he's done and wish he had not whittled her down to nothing, that he had appreciated what he really had. Better to have that regret as small as possible."

"He was just trying to impress you," Martin said. "He didn't mean it like that."

"Moon Rock is just butt hurt cause his girl's letter ain't come through yet," Rasta said as he moved his rook.

While I was focusing on the board Rasta looked at Martin and asked. "How come you speak American?"

"There are more English speakers in India then there are in all of the Americas," Martin said.

"Yeah, but how many of them speak American?" Rasta asked.

126

IIII IIII IIII IIII IIII IIII IIII IIII IIII IIII IIII IIII IIII
IIII IIII IIII IIII IIII IIII IIII IIII IIII

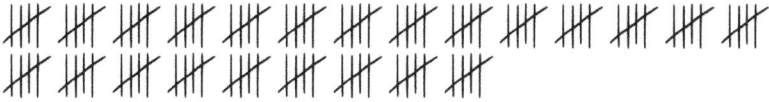

"Wait, none?" Martin asked. "Mother? Father...?" I shook my head.

"Fuck, that's fucked up man. I'm sorry. What about brothers or sisters?"

"Not anymore," I said, suddenly swept up by the feeling of abandonment.

"What do you mean?" he asked. "Dead?"

"Not exactly," I replied. We sat in silence for a moment. My old bunky had transferred out the day before, along with two others in our pod. I had moved to the bottom bunk and Martin quickly had moved to my cell, claimed the top bunk, delighted to be with someone else that had been to college.

"Sorry man," he softly said.

"What about you?" I asked.

"My mom, and my dad, you know, but mostly my mom. She sends me a letter every couple of days, and I call her ever week, but it's really hard man. She is convinced that I didn't do anything. Keeps on telling everyone that everything is going to be alright, that God knows I'm innocent." He shifted his position. He was on the floor, leaning against the wall. I was sitting cross-legged on my bunk. "Shit man, everything was going so smoothly," he added.

"Tell me more about Embry Riddle," I said, trying to steer him towards a more comfortable conversation. "What was it like there?"

"Oh you know, you were in college, lots of hot girls, classes, homework, and wannabe pilots everywhere."

"Did you want to be a pilot?" I asked.

"I don't know. I wanted to be something, you know, to make a difference or do something that mattered, but I don't know if pilot was my thing."

"What is your thing?" I asked.

"Well I always felt like I was supposed to be an actor, you know?" He looked down, the rush of disappointment coursing his face. "But that isn't going to happen anymore."

The room went quiet for a few seconds, full of unpleasant truth.

"You know the worst part man?" he said. "My parents were so proud of me, and my mom..." He stopped talking trying to keep his tears back, but then the tears came anyway.

"I couldn't tell them that I was going to fail some of my classes. I had taken a night job that was barely paying anything at all, took up all of my studying time, shit. My parents borrowed money just to get me there, you know? I couldn't tell them. Then I met this cool guy from the UAE. He knew everybody, all the girls, all the popular kids. We started hanging out all the time, you know? At first, I thought he had so much money because he was from the UAE, you know, rich parents, rich country, but then one night he told me that he was a sort of business man, like it was a secret that he was letting me in on. Then he invited me to help him expand the business, said I was his best friend and the only one he could trust to be part of it. So I quit my shitty job, started making lots of money, and then... well then I ended up here."

His was speaking softly, as if it was simply a wretched dream that he might soon wake up from.

"It wasn't even a couple of weeks man," he said all choked up. "They arrested us on campus, both of us, right there in front of everyone. Stupid, fucking stupid," he said as he wrestled his mistakes for the thousandth time.

We sat in silence together as he reclaimed his composure. A minute passed then he asked, "What about you? What was it like at NASA?"

With an aching sigh I said, "It was paradise." Watching me relax into the ever-receding past, he patiently waited for my reminiscing thoughts to be shaped into words.

"I woke up next to the most beautiful woman every morning," I started. "She was a gorgeous sylph-like biology genius that I couldn't ever get enough of. The alarm would go off and we just started making love, passionately absorbing each other until one more second would make us late for work. Then we would take a thirty second shower, her body glistening between my soapy hands, throw our clothes on and rush off to work. We'd set the alarm earlier each day, but still ended going until that last second anyway." Martin visibly relaxed into the image of my words, encouraging me to continue.

"I would run all kinds of red lights trying to make it to the NBL in time to get cleared by medical, and when I didn't make it on time I'd go to this one cute doctor to get my clearance."

"The NBL?" Martin asked with marked interest.

"The Neutral Buoyancy Laboratory," I said. "Its where they have full sized mock-ups of the International Space Station, the Cargo Bay of the Space Shuttle, and the Hubble Telescope in a giant pool, and the astronauts get in their space suits attached to umbilicals, floating around and practicing their EVA's, or spacewalks."

"Why did you have to get medical clearance?" he inquired.

"Everyone getting in the pool had to be cleared each day," I replied, "so they had a baseline, to make sure you were healthy, trying to keep you from getting the bends, or anything like that." He nodded in a way that encouraged me to share more.

"So then my dive partner, who was an astronaut's son, and I would dress out, and get into the pool with our Nitrox tanks, photographing the module set ups, the astronauts, or whatever." I paused to recall how it felt to sail past the end of a module of the Space Station, letting my imagination believe that I was forever lost in the vast sparkling darkness, slowly adrift.

"When we got out of the pool we'd go to the showers, which were futuristic enough to give the Jetsons a run for their money."

"What do you mean," he interrupted, delighted to be escaping the gravity of his regrets.

"Well," I started with a cracked voice of elation, "the pressure and temperature were completely controllable from an electronic panel inside the shower. And you could select any kind of shampoo or conditioner from the same panel. There were programs for scalp massages, or body massages... it was unbelievable. But the craziest part was the towel at the end. I'd step outside of the shower and this hot towel would just pop out of the wall in front of me, all steaming. I don't know if there was some pressure sensor or what, and I don't know where the towel came from, but it was just right there when you needed it."

"Shit, I wish I was there right now," he said, trying to conjure up enough imagination to teleport there.

"Then I'd call Kaydee," I continued, "and catch up on each other's days. We talked every day, for almost an hour. And we were doing great at being friends, despite the break up. She was even supportive of my relationship with Tiffany." He patiently nodded.

"After medical cleared me to leave, Tiffany would meet me for lunch somewhere, delighted to see me, overflowing with excitement for all the plans we were making. Then we'd both go back to work. I'd either go back in the water, or help with some other Flight Lead duties, but I never turned down an excuse to get into the pool."

"That sounds lovely," he said, still trying to actualize the details around himself.

"Tuesday nights were for volunteer firefighting, Wednesdays for sailing, Thursdays, indoor rock climbing, and every weekend I orchestrated a camping adventure for everyone."

"I thought you were a physicist?" he commented, less slumped, like he was becoming a real person again.

"Yes," I responded, "Started as an astrophysicist, then a geo-astrophysicist, but for my last tour I got the coveted Flight Lead spot in the pool."

"There it is," he said with a sense of satisfaction as he pointed at me.

"There what is?" I asked.

"You, relaxing, finally letting go and opening up to me. I was wondering how long it would take." His directness caught me slightly off guard. "So?" he continued.

"What?" I softly replied, hopefully searching his eyes for a safe place I had almost forgotten.

"Want to give me the real deal? Start from the beginning. Tell me what's up with the whole 'dead, not dead' family story, and the whole Kaydee/Tiffany thing." His eyes were fortified with the patience of having nothing else to do.

"Sure," I said, needing to share far more than he needed to hear. "I grew up in a 'dig your heels in' obstinately devout Mormon family," I started, "with seven siblings, three with Cystic Fibrosis and one with Cerebral Palsy." He gave me the 'are you really going to make me ask' look.

"The first one's a genetic disease that causes respiratory and pancreatic malfunction, and the second is brain damage caused by premature birth that results in impairment of motor function," I said. He nodded, encouraging me to pour it all out.

"My father regularly recounted his glory days of wrestling, proud of the violent streak that he felt made him a man. His permanently furrowed face regularly scowled at me for rooting for the underdog, or nursing a sick kitten back to health. A real man, according to him, didn't waste time on the weak. He was a proud dictator, alone in the world, and weighed down by unfathomable responsibilities.

My mother, on the other hand, was silent and passive. Her inner world was never shared with me. There were no bonding secrets with either of them, no embraces of compassion, only institutional overseeing eyes." I paused for a moment, trying to sort all the details for someone that didn't grow up in that world.

"My siblings and I were regularly reminded, with an unnervingly deep funeral inflection that "Children are to be seen, not heard". Friends were not just subject to parental approval, they were chosen for us. TV was restricted to Little House on the Prairie, Highway to Heaven, and Mormon Conference. There were no video games, only farm chores. The very passage of time seemed to depend on replacing dangerous laughter with the safety of invisible silence." He leaned forward, elbows on knees, keeping his eyes patiently fixed on me.

"Beyond loving my pets, I did not feel particularly outstanding at anything. I was fascinated with maps, but unable to hope for far off adventures. I had been taught that dreams were for the selfish and the greedy. This, coupled with the burning knowledge that my existence was an enormous financial burdened on my parents, left me feeling guilty for even having desires." Martin nodded in a way that let me know that something in his past resonated with that feeling.

"At the age of eight, I accidently discovered masturbation—while trying to pull myself up the soccer goal posts, in order to get big muscles so girls would like me, a consequence I imagined would render me less of a social target to bullies." I paused, trying to gauge if he really wanted all these details. He didn't seem phased.

"Gripping the pole between my legs as I tried to climb, I exerted myself and felt a funny tingling. Later, I discovered that my hand could cause a similar effect. After that, I learned that touching myself like that meant I was going to hell. I repented over and over on this account, confessing to my bishop several times, being directed to wear a thick rubber band and pull it every time I had a sexual thought.

I watched the clock ceaselessly for years, with a bright red wrist, believing that I was the only person in the world with this 'problem'.

I started dating Kaydee in high school, and immediately had to hide the seriousness of our relationship from my family. She came from what my parents considered a 'lesser' family, one with a rumored history of alcohol and drug use, loud motorcycles, and, gasps in horror, divorce. The fact that she was only half Caucasian (and half Persian) was beneath my parents' direct mention, making the loudness of their disapproval unmistakable.

After being together for a year and eleven months, just before I was to leave on my two-year mission, Kaydee and I made love for the first time in the back of her car. It was beautiful, until it was over, at which point we were immediately buried under an avalanche of Mormon guilt. We anxiously deliberated, and eventually decided to gamble our immortal souls against the consequences of being caught.

The plan was simple, but risky. We would lie about having sex. I would go on my mission, return to marry her in two years, and then we would move to a new Ward where we would finally repent, escaping being discovered by our families. If either of us died before that plan played out, we'd both go to hell for eternity.

On my mission, the lie weighed me down. One by one, I confided in each companion, sharing this sensitive secret. To my surprise, each of them reciprocated, revealing that they too were going to hell for the same reason.

Peculiarly, my justification of the lie was different from theirs. I was primarily afraid of my family disowning me. They were just afraid of socially being denied their right of passage. They assured me that my family wouldn't really disown me if they found out. At first, this infuriated me. Why weren't they listening to me? But after the eighth companion independently advised the same, I figured that I must be wrong.

With that threat undermined, I rationally weighed my options and decided that I no longer wanted to carry the lie around with me. I went to my mission president and confessed, hoping he would give me a way to repent and stay on my mission. He called the church leaders, who determined that I was to be sent home. "No longer worthy to serve God" was the phrase they passed along to me." I had to take a moment to distance myself from the sting of the memories.

"Upon my return, I received a prompt and flagrant shunning, forbidden to see, or communicate with, my siblings in any way. I was to leave the house before six in the morning and not to return until after ten at night, at which point I was to go straight to the basement, restricted from entering my old room. As soon as possible, I was to 'make it right' by getting married.

The day before my wedding, while my dad was at work, Kaydee and I broke the no contact rule to inform my family about the wedding plans. When we entered the house, my siblings froze as if we were ghosts that would only go away if they pretended that they couldn't see or hear us.

After several minutes, my mother broke the uncomfortable silence by asking my bride to be, "Why are you marrying him? You deserve so much better." I could feel the pit in my stomach feeding off the awkward shame that was pulsing through my body, sprouting painful its crippling roots. Kaydee tightened her fists and fought her urge to respond.

With everyone else in the room still pretending they couldn't see or hear us, my mom looked directly at me for the first time in months and flatly intonated, "Can we talk?"

My lungs filled with hope. Was 'making it right' going to mean that I would be allowed back into the family?

She led me away from our audience, stopping in front of the faded upright piano, whose keys had stolen much of my childhood. She stood there like she was second guessing herself for an emotional eon, blinking at me through silent tears. I tried my best to use my body language to encourage her next words, any words, desperate for her approval. Tears slowly crept down her face, warmed by the kind of pity religious people feel for nonbelievers. When she finally spoke, she said, "When you die, will you blame how you turned out on me?"

I couldn't keep my composure. I left in a mess of confusion and tears.

Those were the last words I would ever hear from my mother." I swallowed hard, trying to push through the details, but getting stuck.

"Sorry man," Martin said. He looked like he wanted to console me with a hug, but reconsidered in response to the surroundings and how it might be misinterpreted.

"For appearances, my whole family attended my wedding," I continued, "without ever looking me in the eye, or saying a word—expect for the excessive throat clearing my dad made after the bishop said, "Speak now or forever hold your piece."

Then the entire tone of life changed," I said, lightning up. "Although Kaydee and I didn't have much, we had each other and the whole world to discover together. I went to college, but quickly dropped out to pay the bills. I took a job as a construction worker, building homes, while she worked as a dental assistant.

As the novelty of learning heavy machinery, cement work, framing, roofing, wiring, plumbing and finish work subsided, my anxiety about what I was going to do with my life ate at me. I wanted a life of discovery, exploration, and wonder. I wanted to touch the edge of experience, capture the soft echoes of infinity, and make them dance in Kaydee's eyes. But I didn't know how to translate that feeling into a course of action.

Eventually, my angst led me to the university career library where I memorized every detail in the folder titled 'Astronaut', and became enchanted by the dream of standing on Mars. Colored by this aim, all of my talents, hobbies, and interests suddenly had context.

With newfound passion, I rushed home on my bike and told Kaydee about my plan. I was going to study physics, astronomy and geology, get my pilot's license, become SCUBA certified, and learn how to read the barren landscape by mining for gemstones and fossils. I could hardly contain my excitement.

As I finished sharing the sketch of my new dream with my rambunctious bride, I realized how stupid it was for a disowned farm boy to think he had a chance of becoming an astronaut. I looked down in embarrassment and heartbreak. Kaydee reached out, lifted my face and said, "Does this mean I need to get another job?" It didn't even occur to her that I might not have what it takes to become an astronaut. She was completely behind me, so much so that she was already imagining what she could do to help me accomplish all of that.

Her support transformed a fickle echo of what I might become into an insight of what I already was. Through her eyes, I discovered parts of me that had never been unleashed. And once that was out of the bag, well let's just say that my space ship was sleekly designed to run off of high-octane curiosity.

I revitalized the observatory at the University of Utah, founded the astronomical society, became its president, gave birth to weekly public star parties and got hired by the physics department to run them. I majored in physics, geology, geophysics and anthropology. I became an active dinosaur hunter with the Utah Museum of Natural History, earned my SCUBA license and my pilot's license, and any weekend that wasn't spent digging up dinosaurs with the paleontologists was spent with Kaydee exploring the wild west, mining for bixbyite and topaz, camping in dessert, sleeping under the stars, mountain biking, and filling in the map.

On Valentine's Day, we drove off into the sunset, scouting out the route from Salt Lake City to San Francisco, which we were going to do by mountain bike to raise money for the Cystic Fibrosis Foundation. Shaking myself out of a road trance, I mentioned that I had been thinking about our past, and I no longer believed we had done anything immoral by making love before we got married. In fact, I thought it was beautiful. To my surprise she agreed—despite the implications of holding this view.

"So what, are we not Mormon any more?" she asked, with her trademark acceptance.

My whole body pulsed with novel excitement, as possibilities I didn't know I was being held back from slipped inside my horizon of potential. "I guess not," I replied.

She absorbed this monumental shift for a few seconds and then cheerily said, "Let's go buy some real underwear."

"Real underwear?" Martin asked.

"Yeah, Mormons have magic underwear," I said rolling my eyes. "Trust me, its as stupid as you're thinking." He cracked a smile.

"From there we got more and more bold with our honesty. We could now afford to stare our ignorance in the face and explore our curiosities, without shielding ourselves from the truth that exploration might lead to. There was breathtaking freedom in this process of discovery, emotional absorption, and transformation. But nothing was more freeing than being able to honestly discuss our sexual attractions, our fantasies and fetishes, teasing apart the subtleties of our feelings of inadequacies, and fears of rejection.

We intentionally primed new exotic permutations, bonding more and more over the richness of our acceptance. Chasing tiny new details became an erotic art, different people, different interactions, more people, same fetish, but with a new twist, at a swinging party, back home with us... nothing was beyond the shield of our connection."

"Wait," Martin finally interjected. "Are you saying that you two..." I raised an eyebrow, waiting for him to finish. "You know, with others, even though you were married?"

"We didn't cheat on each other if that's what you're asking," I said. "Cheating requires lies, and we had no secrets between us."

"But you did," he finished his sentence with the subtleties of his facial expression.

"Yes we did," I said. "It was beautiful. In fact," I added with conviction, "growing past the nagging anchor of jealousy, learning compersion, delighting in the pleasure of my lover, and daring to bare every facet of myself to her... seriously expanded my mind and potential. As a consequence, my intellectual capacities skyrocketed.

Nature's profound mysteries began to captivate me, and school became easier and easier. Questions captured my imagination. What is magnetism? How do particles get their mass? Why do we have four forces? What is spacetime? Does the universe obey a deterministic evolution law? What is consciousness?" Martin seemed to be still wrestling with the idea of a fully honest adult relationship, but also wanted to see where else I was going to take him, so he didn't interrupt.

"I applied for a co-op position at NASA, got accepted during the same week I finished my pilot's license and was approved for a mining expedition in Peru. Everything was lining up.

For two years, I lived in blissful chase of my dream, going back and forth between the Johnson Space Center in Houston and the University of Utah. But then the honesty had propelled my explorations came with its first difficult hiccup. Kaydee became enthralled with a different path—becoming a model. Days in the gym, clubbing nights, loud music, and unfamiliar substances. On top of this, she was no longer sure that she wanted to live in Texas. There was talk about her moving to California for her dream. Supporting her meant a fork in the road.

We discussed all kinds of ways to redefine the parameters of our relationship, how to continue supporting each other's goals without cutting off our own, but no solution we found felt completely right.

At the start of my third tour at NASA, I was racked with uncomfortable unknowns. My relationship with Kaydee was in limbo, not officially broken up, not officially together, both open to figuring it out. She stayed in Utah, trying to figure things out on her end, while I was in Texas training astronauts, diving into anything that could viscerally satisfy my intellectual curiosities and craft a healthy space for the unknowns in my life.

Then, on a ferry to Galveston Island I met Tiffany. And, in the interest of brevity, I'll just say that I was completely dumbstruck by unexpected attraction."

"So Kaydee knew about Tiffany?" he asked with a hint of confusion.

"Of course," I replied. "Kaydee and I talked on the phone every day, about how I felt about Tiffany, about how she felt about her date the night before. I desperately wanted to support Kaydee's dream without bringing any dead weight to it. At the same time, somehow I already wanted to be able to give Tiffany the moon, figuratively and... well also literally. So... I started imagining doing something that would allow me to do both.

Tiffany could see the wheels in my head spinning. When she confronted me about what I was up to, I spilled the beans. I knew her reply would probably be, "That's crazy! Why would you take that kind of risk?" But I told her anyway.

As I revealed my scheme she looked at me in her special way, the way that made me wish I could live forever in continuous replay of her embrace, desperate to be just a little bit closer. When I finished laying out my fantasy plot, she said, "That's so romantic."

Those words ran through me like a tidal wave. Suddenly I had access to a dream bigger than being an astronaut, a chance to be the romantic dream of her life, in a way that would be beyond erosion.

The next thing I knew we were both pulling off the heist—she wouldn't have me doing it alone. It was a high-adrenaline ordeal, involving a rather persistent replaying of the Mission Impossible theme song in my head as I maneuvered the safe out of NASA's Building 31 North, into a Jeep Cherokee we borrowed.

It took everything in me to calmly drive off the compound, past the guarded gate, without exceeding the unbelievably low speed limit. As we turned onto Saturn Drive we let out an excited scream and then took a beeline to a pre-prepped hotel room, where we sawed open the safe, and cataloged our celestial booty.

We were now collectively in possession of a quarter of a pound of lunar samples. There were fragments from every lunar mission, even a small piece of the first rock picked up by Neil Armstrong on history's most profound day.

The safe had been designated for contaminated samples, ones that had been scientifically tested (heat treated, exposed to chemical reactions, etc.) and returned. As a consequence, each of them bore one of three labels: 'trash', 'consumed', or 'used'. But to us, their sentimental value would always render them priceless.

We drove to Florida to sell some of the samples to a black market buyer. We imagined that we were cashing in a ticket for a future of exciting scientific research, unfettered by the droning grant process and vampire politics that sucks the progress out of science. She was going to discover a new species in Africa, with properties to cure cancer, I was going to revitalize Einstein's dream of making sense of the universe.

Halfway to Florida, we stopped for the night to sleep, but ended up sleeping in a church parking lot, because we couldn't afford a hotel room both nights— despite having the world's most valuable treasure in the trunk.

When we got to Orlando, we got a room and made love, adrenaline still high, full of wild possibilities. I got out of the shower before her, saw the tackle box containing our symbols of love, and put some under the pillow fold in our bed, thinking it would be nice to just hold each other on top of the moon. She came out of the shower and stood in front of me, her perfect runner's body glistening. Cuddling became much much more.

The meeting was held in an Italian restaurant on International Drive. Turns out that every person in the restaurant was an undercover federal agent, the greeters, the wait staff, even the cooks. I felt something was off, but pushed through anyway, not wanting my fears be the reason it all went south. I figured that if I was caught, then I was already caught, on the other hand, if my buyer was worried about me being a threat, it was best to play it cool and not end up getting shot.

After the negotiations had been made, we drove back to the hotel, where the moon rocks were stashed, to make the trade. And then, the shit storm hit."

...

"Count time, count time, count time!" the officer yelled through the slot. After our cells were locked shut, a female officer in her late thirties entered through the sally port and began making the rounds, looking in through each window and counting us with her little clicker.

She approached our cell. I heard two clicks and then she moved on.

Half a minute went by and she said, "Everything okay in there?"

From my bed, I repositioned myself trying to look out the little window in the door, but I couldn't see her. Another fifteen seconds passed and she said, "Just making sure." Then the sound of keys hitting thighs continued.

After she finished counting the second floor she returned through the sally port and then the doors popped back open. Martin climbed back down to continue our conversation. Before we got going Rasta stood in the doorway beaming.

"Ahhh boyyyy, dat was some shit!" he said as he slapped his fingers fervently, over and over.

"What are you talking about?" I asked, thinking it had something to do with her pause outside.

"Check it," he said as he entered my cell. "Dat lady CO be countin' right? So I'm in my cell all by myself, looking through the window and see her in the port, so I step back and pull down my pants right and start going to town." He starts air stroking to help paint the mental image.

"I's spectin her to say something right, but naw, 'stead she plays along, watching me with a smile, giving me the eye. Then she says, "Everything alright in there to buy her some more time. I was look'n right at her when I shot it all out. It was so hot!"

"She would have taken you to C-pod," Martin insisted.

"I'm telling you my niggas, she was into it."

We were clearly unconvinced.

"Fine niggas, you ain't gots to believe me, but I'm telling ya, dat bitch is into it." He sat down next to Martin, apparently unaware that we were in a private conversation.

Changing the subject, Martin aimed a question at us both, "How much time are you looking at?"

"Shiiiiit," Rasta said. "My lawyer spitting some shit about a ten piece, but prolly moe like three or foe, know what I'm sayin'?" Martin looked at me.

"According to the Federal Sentencing Guidelines I'm looking at up to thirty-seven months," I said, trying not to sound forlorn about that much wasted time. "But my lawyer isn't really telling me much."

"What 'bout you Dots?" Rasta asked.

"My lawyer said ten years, or two if I cooperate," Martin replied.

"Shit, so you gonna rat? I hate rats."

"I'm not a rat," Martin said. "But my lawyer has been saying that my codefendant, who is the main guy, is singing like a songbird, trying to put all the blame on me."

"Shit, dat's the game dog. Fucking rats get all the cheese, know what I'm saying?" Rasta said.

"What about you?" I asked Rasta in an attempt to change the conversation. "What are you going to do when you get out?"

"What you mean?" he snapped.

"I mean, what are your plans for your life when you get out?"

"Shit dawg, a nigga can't be messin' his head up with bull shit worries like dat. Got's to be in the here and now, know what I'm sayin'? Ain't nothin' good waiting for a nigga on the outs, know what I mean?"

"You don't even think about it?" I asked.

"What do you care anyway? You got one of them pretty white bitches out there, waiting on you, fancy job flying spaceships and shit, you got your whole life ahead of you soon as you bounce up out of here."

I wondered how he could possibly not know that no girl was ever really going to love a two-time loser, a divorced, convicted felon. He squinted his eyes as he studied my face.

"Ahhh hell naw," Rasta said. "College boy like you? Ahh shit." He leaned forward, tapped me on the shoulder and softly said, "I didn't know my nigga. How long has it been?"

"How long has what been?" I asked.

"Since your shortie sent you a letter?" he replied.

I closed my eyes, trying to distance myself from the topic.

"Shut the fucking door. You mean all dis time? Holy fuck nigga, how long you been down now and she ain't sent you one god damn letter? You gotta drop that shit dawg. Drop it like it's hot."

"She has her reasons," I said, quickly rising to her defense.

"Yeah, reason is she don't love you Moon. Stop torturing yourself and cut that bitch loose. You can't ride this shit like that," he said. "You's looking at doing some hard time you keep waiting like that, always staring out dat glass, thinkin' today's the day you getting that letter. That's the slowest kind of time a man can do, feel me?

Two rules in dis place my nigga." He held up his index finger. "Never take a gift from anyone, shit's always got strings, and" he lifted another finger, "Do your own time. Dey ain't in here man, you got's to let em' go, let it all go."

"She's not a bitch," I said forcefully, eyes flaring.

"My bad dawg, my bad. Just calling it like I sees it," he said with his hands in the air. He looked at Martin, "What about you Dot Boy? You got a shortie on the outs or," he squinted his eyes a bit, "is you one of them fudge packers?" He snickered to himself.

Martin tried to ignore him.

"I knew it," he said as he backed away. "You is one of dem faggots, I knew it."

"I'm not gay," Martin said. "I just don't have a girlfriend."

Rasta was sobviously uncomfortable. "You know all dem dick munchers is going to hell right? Says so in the Bible."

Martin turned towards me like he was about to ask me a question, but Rasta wasn't going to be ignored.

"You do read the Bible... you is a Christian right?" Rasta asked.

"I'm a Muslim," Martin said.

"What? Like one of dem terrorist?" Rasta said. He started moving around on his feet. "And you's only getting two to ten years? Oh hell naw, dat ain't right."

"I'm not a terrorist," Martin said, trying to keep his voice calm.

"But you admit that you're a devil worshiper, dat you don't read the Bible," Rasta said.

"What?" Martin asked. He was clearly feeling the tension in the air, and Rasta's poor logic wasn't making things very comfortable.

"Rasta," I said. He continued intensely looking at Martin. "Hey, Rasta." I waited until he looked me in the eyes, meeting him with a measured gaze. "Not all Muslims are terrorists, in fact, the vast majority of terrorism throughout history has been committed in the name of Christianity, but you're not a terrorist are you?"

"What?" he asked.

"Just like," I said slowly, giving him a chance to see the flaws in his statement, "you being a Christian doesn't make you a terrorist, Martin being a Muslim doesn't make him a terrorist."

"Fuck naw, I ain't no terrorist. I'm a Christian," Rasta said looking back at Martin, the tension in his body demonstrating a high level of threat, as if violence would be the only resolution to his imagined problem.

"Hey Rasta," I said. It was difficult to get him to respond to me. "Martin isn't a terrorist. He was just born in a different part of the world. But look, he even came over here to go to school and learn from our country."

Rasta backed out of the cell, keeping his eyes fixed on Martin, as if he believed that with enough concentration he would actually cause him to burst into flames.

||||| ||||| ||||| ||||| ||||| ||||| ||||| ||||| ||||| ||||| ||||| ||||| ||||| |||||
||||| ||||| ||||| ||||| ||||| ||||| ||||| ||||| ||||| ||||| ||||| ||

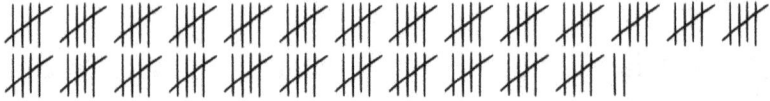

"Roberts!" yelled a voice from the tray slot. I came out of my cell with wide eyes. The Norman Rockwell looking CO winked at me as I approached. "Here you go Professor," he said as he carefully stuffed a pillow through the slot.

"Thank you," I said as I took the pillow with visible gratitude.

He gave me a head nod and covertly signaled with his eyes for me to watch him. He removed a sheet of paper from his clipboard and taped it to the glass. Then he bent down and yelled through the slot. "Bunk assignments. Everyone has until count to be in your assigned bunk."

It was a map of both floors, with names assigned to each cell, signifying upper or lower for specific bunks. My name was in the corner one-man cell on the bottom floor. His kindness appeared genuine, for which I was appreciative, but this exchange was also dangerous, and now that I had a decent bunky, moving to a one-man cell was the last thing I wanted. There was now an immediate threat. To appear to be on the receiving end of preferential treatment from a CO could earn me suspicions of being a snitch. I nodded at him, gently, considered how this new development may paint a target on my back, and went straight back to my cell.

"Did she write you?" Martin asked as he rolled over.

"No," I said. "CO posted bunk assignments. We all have to switch spots." Several inmates were cussing quite expressively, as more and more of them lined up to see the paper.

"Fuck that," a voice out in the pod yelled. "I ain't moving." Martin looked worried and pulled the cover over his head. I began unmaking my bed.

With my bedroll and pillow in my arms, I migrated to my single man cell. Squinty was lying in the bed.

Still clutching my linens, I awkwardly knocked on the door to announce my entrance.

"The fuck you want?" Squinty yelled without actually looking at me.

"The CO posted bunk assignments," I said. "I'm supposed to be in here now."

"Bullshit," he said. "I been in dis cube foe five months now. Ain't no bunk assignments in this fucktard place, never has been." He got up and walked past me. I moved out of the way.

"A hell knaw! Dis is bullshit," a voice yelled.

"Fuck no nigga. Shack me up with a fuck'n pasty ass trailer trash white boy. I ain't fuck'n doing it," another yelled.

Squinty came back to the cell and began grabbing his shit. "Fuck'n white boy privilege."

"I didn't pick this," I said. He looked at me scathingly, his narrowed eyes daring me to give him a reason to take his frustrations out on me.

llll llll llll llll llll llll llll llll llll llll llll llll llll llll
llll llll llll llll llll llll llll llll llll llll llll llll llll

The cells were locked. I sat on the edge of my bed with soft breath, echoes of cinderblock silence reverberating in my head. After several minutes, I started my ever-lengthening yoga routine. I counted the cinderblocks again, adding even the partial blocks as proportional fractions. My count ended on the block that had baked for days and days under my glare. There were many other cinderblocks to gaze at, but this one was just plain, right there in front of my scrutiny, empty of stories, silent. It wasn't waiting to hear from anyone, wasn't anxious to be somewhere else, to be something else. It was just in a single form, void of all other being, free from all angst.

Thirty minutes later, I heard the sally port doors creaking, followed by a CO's call, "Book cart!"

The officer had an inmate pushing the cart for him. They went upstairs first, carrying it together. When they returned to the ground floor, I was one of the last stops. The selection was sparse. I peered through the little window in my door, trying to focus my foggy contacts enough to make out the options of literary distraction. There were only eight books left. All of them looked like cowboy romance novels, except one, which appeared to be a thick tome, nearly a textbook.

"What's that one?" I asked, gesturing to the book I was interested in.

The inmate said nothing, but passed the book to me through the window and wheeled the nearly barren cart to the next cell. I turned my new friend in hand, a book on ancient Egyptian, written in thirty-third dynasty hieroglyphics. I flipped through it briefly, finding that each hieroglyphic line was translated into Coptic below, and then in English below that—a decoding mystery.

...

The doors were open, but I was still on my bunk, transfixed by the same cinderblock. Squinty causally entered my cell, with a half-finished braid job, holding his commissary cache.

"Hey Moon Rock," he said as he entered my cell. I gave no response, not even to acknowledge his presence. He sat down on my bunk unceremoniously, intentionally putting his leg close to mine. "Noticed you never get any commissary." He reached in his bag and pulled out a bag of pork rinds, as if it were a treat from his Christmas stocking. Then he presented them to me saying, "If you need a friend... I can be a friend to you." He placed his other hand on my knee. I offered no response, unwilling to give even a thought to his game.

"I can take care of you every week, know what I'm talk'n 'bout?" he said as he shook the bag in front of me, signaling for me to take it. I continued to ignore him, focusing past the bag to the spot I'd come to fixate on. He began sliding his hand further up my leg. I saw only the cinderblock.

He stood up abruptly in frustration, which quickly turned to sullen disappointment, then prickly anger. "Oh, so you're too good to be friends with me, huh? Is dat how it is?" He stood directly in my line of sight, but I kept my eyes distantly focused.

"This is why you don't have any friends Moon Rock," he yelled in imagined offense. He put his pork rinds back into the bag, leaned in testily, and said, "Shit Moon Rock, you wouldn't know a friend if he was staring right in your muthafuckin' face." Then he left in a huff, slapping his plastic sandals loudly on the floor with each step. I continued breathing slowly with deserted eyes.

Minutes later, he came back into my cell with a far more insidious motive. Without any warning, he rushed in and went right for my face, glancing me crookedly in the jaw. My trance ended. Seconds later, I had him pinned on his back, using my weight to wrestle him down. Several people were crowding the door to my room, but left us enough space to flail around.

"Are you done yet?" I asked, annoyed with his very existence, as I jabbed him hard in the ribs with my elbow. He squealed but didn't reply. I jabbed him again to provoke a response.

"Ok, ok," he wheezed.

"You gonna start any more shit?" I asked, poised menacingly to elbow him again.

"We cool. We cool," he said. I pushed off of his surrendered body, cautiously watching. He slowly regained his feet with obvious embarrassment and confusion, but didn't attempt another swing. After he left, most of the assembled crowd thinned out, except Rasta, Comb-over, and Martin.

"You could have kicked the shit out of him Moon!" Rasta said with excitement as he shoved past Martin.

"And then what?" I asked, the anger cooling to melancholy. "Go to the hole?"

. . .

I reached under my mattress and pulled out the sheets of lined notebook paper I had acquired from Mr. Windy City. Sitting in the middle of my bunk cross-legged, I continued my hieroglyphic decoding quest. The silence of my empty cell and the pictographs were boon companions. There were phonetic characters, action characters, and context characters. For example, if a phonetic combination represented a name, then it was encircled with a bubble, like a box with rounded edges. One end of this bubble had a line signifying which end to start reading the name from. And if the name belonged to a female, then a little egg followed the phonetic characters within the bubble.

Endless hours behind that locked door transformed into something else, until my focus was broken.

꜀꜀꜀꜀꜀꜀꜀꜀꜀꜀꜀꜀꜀꜀꜀
꜀꜀꜀꜀꜀꜀꜀꜀꜀꜀꜀꜀꜀꜀꜀
꜀꜀꜀꜀꜀꜀꜀꜀

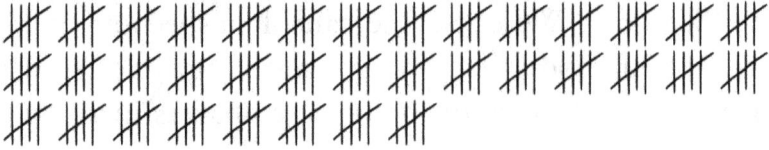

"Your move," Frizz said. We camped on the polished cement floor beneath the stairs. All the metal tables were taken.

Suddenly a strange ruckus arose. At first, it wasn't clear what was going on. Simultaneous shouts prompted everyone to rise to their feet. Several spectators took on the tones of encouragement for a dogfight. All eyes were focused in one direction. My stomach tightened as I realized it was in the direction of Martin's cell. I pushed my way through the crowd just in time to see Martin flying out, landing on his side on the cement in a thick grunt. I watched him scramble to get back up, in either valiance or self-preservation. Rasta rushed out after him, raging with fury and overflowing with incoherent screams. His foot sought to make contact with Martin's torso again and again.

I pushed through the crowd and latched onto Rasta, pulling him away from Martin. "It's not worth it man," I said with my arms around him in a protective bear hug, attempting to pull him away from Martin's injured form. He was breathing hard, seeing red, but wasn't fighting hard to get out of my restraint. I wheeled him around so both of our backs were to Martin. Instead of retreating, Martin scrambled to his feet and lunged forward and viciously ripped an entire fist full of dreadlocks out of Rasta's scalp.

While howling in pain, Rasta escaped my hold and began a relentless onslaught of pounding fists. Martin fought back but didn't land any prominent punches. It looked as if Rasta was going to kill Martin, each fist making dull thuds as they found places to injure.

"Stop it!" I yelled, trying to get between them. Neither of them were hitting me, so I kept pushing myself between them.

"Lock down!" a CO yelled through the slot as several other officers started the transfer into the pod. Nobody moved until the second door of the sally port began to open. All but the three of us darted to their cells. The officers came in with a mission. They grabbed Rasta, examined Martin's hands and face, and then told both Martin and me to return to our cells.

After all cells were secured, the officers loaded Rasta into the sally port. Preacher began to sing. It was quiet at first, but then grew louder and louder.

"Another one bites the dust, hey. Another one bites the dust. And another one's gone, another one's gone, another one bites the dust." By the third round of this tune many people were enthusiastically joining in.

Two hours later, the doors were popped open. People poured out of their cubes like nothing had happened, nonchalantly returning to their practiced exercises in futility. Preacher leaned on the railing upstairs, apparently waiting for a public interface with me. When I was in clear view he began to yell.

"Hey, hey!" He pounded his fists on the railing, echoing throughout the pod. Everyone in the room went solemnly quiet. "A fight is a fight. We respect dat in dis pod." He stood tall, leading with the imposing barrel of his chest as if the occupied even more space than he already did. "From now on, two men start a fight, dey finish it. Anybody stops a fight, and dey deal with me!" He looked directly at me. There was no question if the threat was real. I let out a measured exhale and tried to imagine the volatile collection of childhood issues he was still nursing. Then I went into Martin's cell.

Martin was sitting on his bunk, with his hands cupped together.

"Fighting isn't really my thing," he said when he finally looked up at me, bravado faded. "Just too small." I sat down with my back to the wall, facing him.

After a minute of silence I asked, "So, what was that all about?"

"Nothing," he said. "Just happened." He opened his hands and revealed the collected coup of dreadlocks.

"Did you still have that in your hands when the CO's were checking you?" I asked in surprise.

"No, picked it up after," he said with a smile. "At least I got him back a little." He trailed off, I knew there was something else on his mind.

"Are you going to tell me what's up with you?" I asked.

He sat quietly, shifting his position slightly.

"Talked to my mom," he said, defeatedly.

160

"And?" I asked softly.

"I had to tell her," he said.

"Tell her what?" I asked.

"That I did it," he responded, emotion rising. "I did what they said I did. She was so confident that I didn't, that her son wouldn't do that, that they were setting me up. But I had to tell her."

"What did she say?" I asked.

He sniffled a little and said, "She said that I should read the Koran and pray and I would be guided back to the path." His teary eyes met mine. "Will you read it with me? My mom says that Allah might have put me in here to share his message with people in here that need it. She says that anyone that reads the Koran and prays for two weeks will hear Allah in their heart."

His face held his plea as I wrestled with the conflict between my desire for him to overcome the morass of religious thinking, and my desire for him to have the support of his loved ones. "I'll do it with you."

Martin proceeded to show me how to pray in his tradition, pulling our pant legs up, washing our feet and our hands clear up to the elbows. Five times a day we prostrated in the prescribed direction, recited the prayers, and then he read the Koran to me.

"You ever worry about getting raped in here?" he asked me one day as we finished the prayer routine.

"Of course," I said. "Beat up by the cops, tortured by the cops, beat up by the inmates, raped by them... who wouldn't worry about that in this situation."

"Yeah, but you're a lot bigger than I am. I worry about it a lot," he said. "A lot of these guys look at me like they... you know, like that, because I'm small, because it would be easy. They call me girl names and then give me that look."

"Does your bunky do that?" I asked.

"No, but some of the guys he hangs out with do," he said with a sigh.

"You're going to be just fine," I said. "Nobody is going to rape you. You just stand your ground if they approach and you'll be ok."

‖‖ ‖‖ ‖‖ ‖‖ ‖‖ ‖‖ ‖‖ ‖‖ ‖‖ ‖‖ ‖‖ ‖‖ ‖‖
‖‖ ‖‖ ‖‖ ‖‖ ‖‖ ‖‖ ‖‖ ‖‖ ‖‖ ‖‖ ‖‖ ‖‖ ‖‖
‖‖ ‖‖ ‖‖ ‖‖ ‖‖ ‖‖ ‖‖ ‖‖ ‖‖ ‖‖ ‖‖ ‖

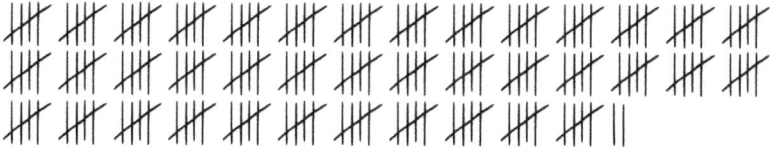

"Service in ten minutes!" yelled a CO.

Martin came over to my cell. "Wanna go?" he asked. I shrugged. "It's at least a chance to get out of here," he added.

"Yeah, wearing cuffs in a small room while some miserable guy short on compassion, looks down at us and preaches about why we're all going to hell for masturbating," I said.

"Well, it's the only way I get to talk to my friend," he said.

"You mean your codefendant?" I asked.

"He's still my friend," he said.

I looked at him with disbelief.

"What?" he asked. "He wouldn't do that. They are just rumors."

I continued the look.

"Anyway, better to ask him about it directly."

The CO shackled and cuffed the four of us inside the sally port. We followed him down the corridor to the chapel, joining up with inmates from other cells. When we reached the door to the chapel, the officer removed our handcuffs but left our leg cuffs on.

It was a medium-sized room with rows of pale wooden benches facing a pulpit and a weathered upright piano. We sat in the middle row. When his codefendant entered the chapel, Martin signaled for him to sit next to him. His codefendant sat in the row behind him instead.

"Does anyone here play the piano?" the Chaplin asked. Nobody responded. I raised my hand.

"Good," he said, "why don't you come up here and play us this hymn so we can get started." Martin and his codefendant began whispering.

I sat down on the wooden piano bench and placed my fingers on the keys. Another life flashed before my eyes, teleporting me to that room with the shaggy red carpet, sunk three steps below the kitchen. I remembered sitting on the bench, in that room, thinking of my secret spot outside. A spot where my ticket to a different life was hidden high in the grapevines along the southern side of the house— seventeen dollars and thirty-five cents wrapped in a plastic bag and stuffed away in a gap between the bricks. Only a few more months and I'd have enough to officially run away. Or so I thought.

"Everyone," the Chaplain said as he banged on the pulpit. The chatter quieted down. "Turn to page one oh eight," he said holding up his hymnbook.

The crowd halfheartedly murmured the words as I played the distantly familiar, yet unnerving song.

"Onward Christian soldiers, marching as to war. With the cross of Jesus, going on before." How had I never objectively analyzed how much hate and bigotry was encoded in even the songs? How had they kept me that blind?

After the singing concluded, I tried to drag my chain back to the center bench, but the Chaplin directed me to sit on the front row—the only person on the front row.

"Today we are going to talk about the Gospels," the Chaplain said. "What the scholars like to call the synoptic Gospels, for some reason."

"It means single view," I said softly. The Chaplain looked at me. I continued, "Because three of the gospels, Matthew, Mark, and Luke, all held one view of Jesus while John tells a completely different and largely contradictory story."

"What?" he asked with a heavily laden tone, meant to convey that prisoners were only allowed to listen.

I didn't respond.

He continued. "The synoptic Gospels tell us about our lord Jesus. We study these gospels because the more we know about our Lord the more we can please Him." He cleared his throat and changed his posture, as if he were awkwardly auditioning for an acting role that required emotional expressions that were beyond him.

"This week I met a young lady, right here in this very facility." He was pointing towards the floor, jerking his hand with the last few words. "A young lady, and I use that word very loosely, that our Lord is very disappointed with." He shook his head to give his empty words the illusion of empathy.

"I explained to her that she was fortunate that God was punishing her for her evil ways, giving her a chance to make amends. But did she accept God's judgment? No, no, no. This whore, who had a baby with a man she was only engaged to, who was caught smoking marijuana by our city's finest, who also, mind you, found another joint in her purse," he pinched his fingers together acting out picking up a joint, "had no interest in repenting." Using both hands he grabbed the pulpit and leaned forward.

"This stubborn, sinful girl wasn't even interested in confessing. All she had were lies, saying that she did nothing wrong, talking about how she needed to be with her baby. But it was too late for that. God's punishment is absolute. She cannot escape His will." He moved in front of the pulpit.

Raising his voice, he continued. "Do you know what she said to that? What did she say to God's loving and holy offer for her to repent? I'll tell you what she said. She spat in my face, in the face of a representative of His Holy Church." He was shaking his outstretched index finger again.

With a lowered volume he looked upward and added, "I can only hope that by granting her enough time in solitary she will come to His graces and repent. For the sake of her immortal soul."

He returned to the pulpit and continued his scripted sermon.

At the end of the sermon, the Chaplin led us in prayer. As heads were bowed, I looked around and tried to observe the rest of the room. People do curious things when they think no one is watching, even in the pursuit of piety. Afterwards I made my way next to Martin as we waited by the door for our handcuffs.

"Well?" I asked. His crestfallen face said it all. "Shit man, I'm sorry," I said.

We were led back down the hallway. "That was weird," Martin said. "Is that what church service is always like?"

"I fucking hate that guy," I said, shaking my head in angry frustration.

"The Chaplin?" he asked.

"Yes." I said. "Total piece of shit! The way he talked about that poor girl."

"Relax," he said in a voice heavy with distraction. "Everything will work out." I didn't want to make things harder on him than they already were, to call too much attention to the suffering that extended beyond the rim of his plate, so I kept the rest of my doom-filled forecast to myself.

HHT HHT HHT HHT HHT HHT HHT HHT HHT HHT HHT HHT HHT HHT
HHT HHT HHT HHT HHT HHT HHT HHT HHT HHT HHT HHT HHT
HHT HHT HHT HHT HHT HHT HHT HHT HHT HHT HHT HHT HHT HHT
HHT HHT I

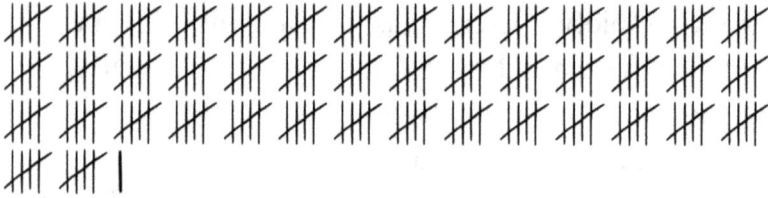

The depths of boredom desperately carried my thoughts. 'Why wasn't there any dust?' I wondered. 'It's not like anyone is cleaning the walls. Especially up high where it's hard to reach. So why isn't there any dust in the cracks between the cinderblocks?' Little paint nodules served as landscape markers, creating a map of an imaginary world in my mind. I scoured the room again, trying to finally decide where I'd have the elves live, and which section should be home to dragons. There were several factors to consider.

"Davis, Hussain, and Williams—transfer. Pack your shit!" yelled a CO, bringing me out of my trance. I stood up, pressed my face against the window in my door, and waited. A few minutes later the officer returned and popped open three doors. Martin came into my view as he approached the sally port with his bedroll in his arms. Two other inmates made their way down the stairs and joined him. As the door cried open, Martin looked my way. He stepped inside, every movement demoralized, but offered me a gentle nod as the portal enveloped him.

...

I knew it was months past Christmas, but the song was in my head and I had to get it out. I began whistling, blowing in and out without pause. After the song was finished, I started a new one. Someone upstairs began singing along. When the officer popped the doors, I was still whistling. I finished the song, then grabbed my tiny bar of soap and my towel and walked to the shower. In the shower, I sang a Latin song I learned in choir. I never knew what it meant, what it was saying, I just liked how it felt to sing.

As I walked back towards my cell, Fat Albert, a big black man with bulging eyes, stepped in my way. "You alright Moon?" he asked.

"Fine," I cynically replied, without really looking at him.

"Cuz you look like you's 'bout to crack. Know what I'm talk'n 'bout?" He lowered himself right into the line of sight of my despondent gaze. "All that whistling 'n shit… singing in the shower… you ain't about to call it quits on us is you, Moon Rock?"

"I'm fine," I said, in monotone.

"You want to talk about it?" he asked gently.

A young black kid that had only been in the pod a few days approached us. "Hey Moon Rock, you gots a radio?"

"No," I said, flatly.

He looked confused. "I heard you playing it earlier," he said.

"I was just whistling," I said.

"You still gots to breathe when you whistle," he

said. Dat was like minutes without breathing."

"I just whistle while breathing in also," I said.

He gave me a strange look. "Can I see it?" he asked.

"See what?" I asked.

"The radio," he said, insistent.

I ignored him and started to move around both of them towards my cell. They both followed.

"Ain't nothing to be 'shamed of you know," Fat Albert said. "White boys almost always crack up in here. Jail just wasn't made for white boys, know what I'm talk'n 'bout? But you?" he made a whistling sound. "Shit, you gots a whole life out der waiting for you."

Fat Albert followed me inside my cell and the new kid stopped at the doorway. "Shit, when you get out you'll be fucking girls in a league the rest of us niggas will never see." His attempt to provide perspective was well meaning but wholly ineffectual.

I sat down and started focusing on the wall. He sat next to me.

"You just gots to clean out dem cob webs in your brain. Know what I'm saying? Got's to let all that shit go dawg."

After looking around my empty room, the kid lost interest and left.

"She still ain't sent you no love?" Fat Albert asked, trying to get me to volley with him.

After several seconds of slouched silence, I quietly said, "It's my birthday today."

Fat Albert took a few breaths and then in a kind

voice said, "I'd say happy birthday, Moon, but I won't do you like that."

In a breath of sullen acquiescence I said, "Life is never going to be the same."

"Damn straight!," he replied. "Ain't never gonna be the same, changes e'ry day. Nigga, white boy, don't matter, none of us fuckas gets a do over, cain't go back, only forward." He twisted his body so that it was facing mine.

"Shit, Moon, you really cain't see how good you gots it huh? You's got anything and everything waiting out there. Shit what was you talk'n bout yesterday— flying the muthafuckin' the Space Shuttle and shit?"

"It was the Space Shuttle Simulator," I said.

"Zactly," he said. "Ain't no muthafuckin' way I could ever do anything like that. Wouldn't even know where to start. Was born poor, gonna die poor."

"I was born poor too," I said. He looked at me incredulously, eyebrow arching.

"Really," I said. "Grew up on a farm, super Mormon parents, seven mouths to feed, four siblings with diseases, always in the hospitals, buying our clothes from the DI. Never had money." He looked at me like I was a forked-tounge politician. "Except for the day I got arrested," I added.

"He scrunched his face in confusion and said, "The DI?"

"It's like Goodwill for broke Mormons," I said.

"You never had money? You worked for NASA," he said.

"Yeah, and I've never had a thousand bucks in the bank. Put everything I had on my dream, paying for school, for pilot's lessons, and equipment for mining, exploring... all so I could be an astronaut that survives on Mars, be the one that figures out how to get out of any disaster that happens, and settle humanity there."

"Shit," he said. "See that's what I'm talk'n 'bout. White boys got no idea what poor is. All that privilege just makes them blind, they can't fuckin' see through it. Never had a thousand bucks in your bank account? Shit, I ain't never had a bank account. Ain't no nigga had a bank account. Too busy trying to survive, not get shot at and shit, know what I'm talk'n bout? A nigga cain't be filling up his head with dreams and shit. Dat shit is for white boys."

I looked at him. "I'm not saying that different starting points don't make things harder. I'm saying that dreaming only changes your life when you dream big." A fleeting wisp of hope animated my voice. "Aiming for little things here and there will never take you anywhere. You have to dream as big as you can imagine, then all the little steps between here and there have meaning and can lead to something great." Despite the twinge of wonder in my statement, he remained unconvinced.

"Seriously," I said. "All you have to do is pick a dream, a big dream, not a little one. The little ones are too difficult to keep your eye on but the big ones capture you and wake you up in the morning ready to go."

"Shit, I already wake up every morning ready to go, know what I'm saying?" He raised up his fist waiting for me to fist bump him, "Huh, huh?" I ignored him.

"I gots you, Moon. I have a dream dat ten bitches be fighting over my meat," he said pointing to his crotch. "Dey just spend der day getting all wet thinking 'bout my rock hard..."

"No, you have to pick something bigger than that," I said.

He thought for a few seconds and then said, "A hundred bitches."

I looked back at the wall with a sigh, and talked more to it than him. "Years ago, I was outside, laying out at night and found an orange, almost red star. I wondered how far away it was, if there was life there, and if there was, what kind of life? I thought about that star, imagining that it was the furthest away thing there was, a place where everything was different. Later I found out that it wasn't a star at all, it was the planet Mars. I asked if there was life on Mars and well you know where that question leads." I was looking past him, talking more to the unreachable past than anything else. He was trying to follow.

"I remembered watching the moon landings, humans on the moon, the first ones to touch the heavens, really going somewhere, looking back on earth in a way no human ever had before and I imagined being the first man on Mars. I got me a poster of the inside of the Space Shuttle and absorbed it every day, memorizing every little detail.

That dream motivated me to get my pilot's license, triple major in physics, geology, and anthropology, dig up dinosaur bones with paleontologists, get SCUBA certified, mine for gems, run the observatory, found the astronomical society... It became my whole life, carried me to places I knew nothing about, opening up my whole world."

"Okay, okay, okay," he said in his 'let me school you back to reality' voice, "all dat shit you spittin' Moon, ain't never been an option for a nigga. Not one." I took a breath, poised to unveil my deep truth, to gift him with the kind of motivation that empowers someone past all the things that could be stacked against them, but the filter of his reality scorched everything I could think to say, leaving me with just ashes in my mouth.

"Hold up Moon Rock," he said, shaking his head in sheer disbelief. "You mean you did all of dat just to get your pasty ass up in space? Shit, white people is stupid," he said still shaking his head. "Why would anybody want to go to space? Ain't no chicken, ain't no pussy, nothing."

I closed my eyes, took a slow deep breath to consider my audience and then remarked, "Perhaps, but think about it this way, if you make it to space, then when you come back you can have all the chicken and pussy you could ever want."

"Shit, dat dreaming big shit might work for white boys, Moon Rock, but a nigga ain't gots nothing but a bullet coming if he starts play'n dat game. Know what I'm talking 'bout? 'Sides, that wasn't your dream," he said.

"What are you talking about?" I said.

"For real, Moon," he replied. "I seen you pacing around and shit. You ain't been up in here worried about not being up there in fucking space. You spend all your worries on your shortie, staring out dat window, waiting on dat letter, think'n 'bout dat pussy. I seen you."

We sat in silence for a few seconds while I weighed the lofty against the near-at-hand.

"Okay, okay," he added as he shifted his weight, "ain't no thing. Check it. You wanted to be the astronaut dealing with all the fucked up shit up der, and now you's in here dealing with the shit down here." He hit me on the shoulder and half-jokingly said, "You's like the jail astronaut now, dealing with dis disaster, on dis fucked up netherworld made of concrete, bars and tears."

His words pushed on a tectonic rift that was subduing my entire world. It didn't matter that the momentum of that subduction was unstoppable. I had to resist the next tremor, to preserve something of the landscape of the past, by making myself rigid and cold. I closed my eyes and tried to imagine the stars as fixtures to hold onto.

"Just think of dis as the dark side of the moon," he added in attempt to be consoling.

We sat quietly for a bit as my mind retraced the past.

"So what's stopping ya?" he asked.

"What do you mean?" I replied.

"If all you need is a big dream, something to believe in and really aim for, what's stopping ya from doing dat now?" He was staring me down with sincerity.

"Its different now," I said, demoralized.

"Ain't no different," he said. "Its still you against the whole world, shooting for the impossible, aiming high. Shit, all dis just makes every dream big, know what I'm talk'n 'bout?" I appreciated his efforts to distract me from the spiraled drain my mind was twisting down, but the deep sense of abandonment pulsing through me left me impervious to such attempts.

His posture began to change. "Let me axe you sometin', Moon," he said. "So you's a Muslim now?"

"What?" I asked. "What are you talking about?"

"I seen you kneeling with that Muslim, reading the Koran, all dat."

"That doesn't mean I'm a Muslim," I said.

"So you's just exploring? Just trying it out?" he asked.

"Not at all," I said, "I'm not religious."

"So if you never believed dat shit, why did you hang out with that Muslim and do all dat?" he asked.

I looked at him, remembering Martin's eyes full of tears when he asked me to pray with him and said, "Because he was alone."

卌 卌 卌 卌 卌 卌 卌 卌 卌 卌 卌 卌 卌 卌
卌 卌 卌 卌 卌 卌 卌 卌 卌 卌 卌 卌 卌 卌
卌 卌 卌 卌 卌 卌 卌 卌 卌 卌 卌 卌 卌 卌
卌 卌 卌 卌 卌 卌 卌 卌 卌 卌 卌 卌 ||

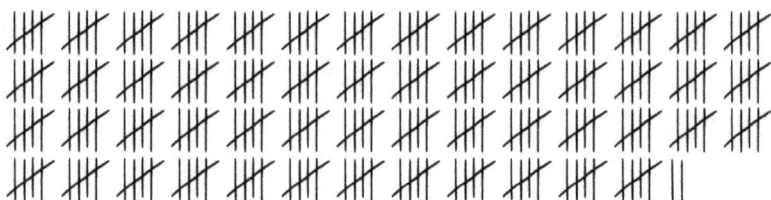

The lights from the pod turned on, spilling into my room from the little window.

"Count!" yelled a female voice. Keys clinked as she made her rounds. When she reached my room, she shone her flashlight on me and clicked her clicker, adding to her body count. The flashlight's beam didn't go away. She was pointing it at my crotch.

"Everything alright in there?" she asked. I looked at her. It was the same CO that Rasta had claimed watched him masturbate. She turned the flashlight around, suggestively highlighting herself for me as she made a circle with one hand and began air stroking. I didn't reply.

"Stand up where I can see you," she said. I stood up and faced her. She pointed the flashlight back at my crotch. "Go on," she added.

I wished I cared enough to play her game. She was attractive enough, and from a different perspective I could imagine thinking that the circumstances added a significant thrill to the exchange, but my practiced callousness left me immune to even this base desire. I looked past her, empty of even the desire to desire.

She eventually grew impatient with my unresponsiveness and said, "I'll check on you next time." Then she continued her rounds.

CHAPTER 4: MOONSHINE

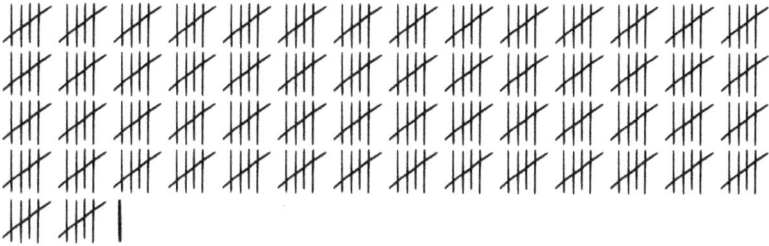

卌 卌 卌 卌 卌 卌 卌 卌 卌 卌 卌 卌 卌 卌
卌 卌 卌 卌 卌 卌 卌 卌 卌 卌 卌 卌 卌 卌
卌 卌 卌 卌 卌 卌 卌 卌 卌 卌 卌 卌 卌 卌
卌 卌 卌 卌 卌 卌 卌 卌 卌 卌 卌 卌 卌 卌
卌 卌 |

Back in chains, scuffing along a polished floor, we followed the young officer in front of us as he talked on his hand radio. "Face the wall," the officer ordered. He motioned for us all to move to the left side of the hallway. "Eyes forward!" he yelled from just behind our heads. "I don't want you looking at anything but concrete, do you understand me?" He began intensely pacing behind us.

We could hear the sound of clinking chains getting louder and louder. "Hell---o ladies," one of the inmates to my right said. The officer walked behind him. "No talking and keep your eyes forward!" he exploded in the way drill sergeants do in second-rate war flicks. Then in an unmistakable female resonance we heard, "Hey boys."

Several girls started whistling faintly as they passed behind us in their chains.

"I'm already handcuffed daddy, you want some of this?"

Other than the occasional female officer, or prosecutor, I hadn't actually seen a female in almost ten months. I had to look. Two of the girls that had already passed us looked back and caught the gaze of my eyes. Even in those county jail outfits the feminine form retained its power. One of them smiled and the other blew me a kiss. I smiled back and turned my head forward again as the officer approached me. He said nothing.

We all squeezed into a small chamber. The officer pushed the button on his hand radio and said, "Sally port twelve." A metallic door with a glass window slowly slid closed trapping us inside. "Clear," the officer said into his radio. Then a metallic and glass door on the other side of the chamber slowly opened. We entered the new hallway. The floors were cement but polished. Several empty 'lawyer visitation' rooms decorated both sides of the hall.

Further down the hallway we came to a large room on the right. "A-Pod," the officer said into his radio. The prison was separated into several different pods. A-Pod was for general population, sort of a mix between different offense levels, but also a mix between federal, state, and county prisoners. This combination gave rise to rumors that it was the most relaxed pod in the facility.

A door electronically slid open, revealing my new universe. This pod was much larger than any I had been in before. Cells stretched around the exterior of the pod in two levels. There were eight four-man cells on the bottom floor and seven four-man cells, plus two showers, on the top floor. Colorless stairs on the left and right sides connected a deck that provided access to the upper level cells. In the center of the pod, there were four rows of stuck together hard plastic chairs, the kind you might find at an airport. These gray seats faced a television, attached to a cement pillar. Eight polished metal tables, with four round chairs were permanently bolted to the cement floor, scattered throughout the room. Four cement pillars had payphones attached to them. Each cell had two bunk beds and a toilet-sink.

The pod officer came out and began removing our chains. "Grab yourself a boat and a bed roll," he instructed. Just inside the door was a pile of plastic mattresses, sheets, blankets, towels and grey plastic containers referred to as 'boats'. These shoddy beds were seven feet long, three feet wide, about ten inches deep, and looked something like a cheap, squared off sit-on-top canoe made out of melted garbage.

After we entered the pod, the door closed behind us. The pod officer walked to his desk and pushed some buttons on his control panel that popped our cell doors open. Next to his desk, I noticed that we could see directly into the showers from where we were standing. The doors were only half doors, starting at knee height, but from the officer's view below the entire interior of the shower was visible.

The pod officer called out two last names. The inmates stepped forward. The officer walked them to their lower level cells and then closed their barred doors. Then he called out two more names, "Roberts! White!" We both followed him. We dragged our boats up the left staircase, making a scraping sound that echoed through the quiet pod. The first cell was mine. I followed the officer's hand motion and stepped inside. He closed the door behind me, dismissing me like a dog surrendered to the pound. The door made a loud metallic click as it closed. The other prisoner was escorted to the other open cell.

My new cell had smooth white walls. Above the toilet-sink was, as seemed to always be the case, another polished piece of metal pathetically masquerading as a mirror. Both of the bunk beds were full. I put my boat down next to the wall of bars and proceeded to put my mattress inside of it and make my bed.

The officer closed the last door and returned to his desk on the ground floor. Murmuring and chatter started filling the air. Loud talkers, punctuating their words like bible thumpers, people banging on their toilets and spitting rhymes, and bits and pieces of softer conversations contributed to the echoes that resonated throughout the chamber.

"It's better the other way around," said a short white man, sitting on the upper bunk to the left. He was completely bald in the middle of his head with long hair on the sides. I looked at him in confusion. "Your boat, flip it over and you'll get a little give when you lay down," he said as he mimed with his hands.

"Thanks for the tip," I said as I flipped the boat upside down.

A very lanky black man was sleeping on the top

bunk closest to the toilet, letting out occasional snorts. His feet were sticking off the bed, hovering right in the space where one's head would be if they were comfortably standing while pissing in the toilet. To make things worse, his feet were appalling. His skin was calloused and cracked and worst of all his toenails looked like they had never been cut. They curled completely around making more than a full circle, each with its own radius, except for the pinky toe, which arched into a half circle and protruded over two inches out.

"Glad they finally put someone in here I can talk to, know what I mean?" my boat-advising cellmate said as he was dangling his feet off his bunk. I looked around the room. "You smoke?" he asked. I shook my head. "Good, more for me," he said, pleased with himself.

He jumped off his bed, making a loud thud on the floor, then stepped into his plastic sandals and sat next to me on my boat.

"So... are you the guy?" he said with a half twisted neck.

"The guy?" I asked.

"You know, the one they have been talking about... with the moon rocks and shit."

"What have they been saying?" I asked, feeling the sandpaper of being reduced to a novelty once again.

"They say that the rocks were worth a hundred million dollars." He waited for a reaction. "Some even say they were priceless, the biggest heist of all time."

"They say a lot of things," I said, not encouraging more of this logic.

"You want to know how I'm going to make my millions?" he asked.

I looked at him with apprehension, not sure where this was going.

"I'll tell you. I'm going to write a book called *How to Get Away with Murder*," he said with a proud look.

"I think you might be overestimating your market," I said.

"What do you mean?"

"Well let's just say that there probably aren't that many people out there that want to grow up as a murderer."

"How do you know?" he asked, dubious.

"Just a hunch," I said.

"You might be surprised," he said as he straightened his posture. "Ain't nobody out there that ain't greedy for power."

"Okay, but how many murderers want to have a book called *How to get away with murder* sitting on their coffee table when the cops come by to question them?"

"They don't have to keep the book once they've read it," he retorted.

"Fair point, but have you noticed a possible trend between literacy and violence?"

"What do you mean?" he asked.

"Well, it seems possible to me that the people that tend to be most violent are also the people that read the least."

"Perhaps you've neglected to understand the truly violent," he said with an air of superiority. "Don't worry, I ain't mad at you. It's a common mistake."

I looked at him unconvinced.

"Sure, there are lots of poor people, who may not know how to read so well that find themselves in bad situations that can lead to having to kill someone, but those people never get away with murder. It's the educated people, the politicians, the lawyers, the powerful people that get away with murder. I've known lots of these guys; hell I've worked for them. And the only reason I'm in here instead of out there like them is that they knew how to play the game already. Hard lessons, but that's what my book is about. It's about playing the game and winning. And I can tell you this," he started wagging his outstretched finger, "there hasn't been a powerful leader, or a really wealthy man in the history of time, that didn't get what he had without murder."

He was growing more and more animated, but despite the topic he didn't give off a threatening vibe. "That's just the way of things. Always has been and always will be. We like to pretend that society is nice and polite, but the people with the best smiles, the people that everyone looks to, are the ones you have to watch out for the most."

He got up to piss and almost walked right into the massive nasty feet sticking out of the bed. He jerked back, exaggerating his disgust with his whole body, then he motioned as though he were starting up a chainsaw, sounds and all. "Reeee-neee-neeee-neeeee," he gestured as he pretended to cut the toenails off with his imaginary weapon.

He leaned forward with one hand on the wall and began pissing. "By the way, I'm John."

"Tell me John," I said as I focused on the fixture of irony in our cell, "what's the deal with the window?"

"What do you mean?" he asked as he pulled off some toilet paper to wipe the toilet down.

The window in our cell was eight inches wide and went from two feet above the ground to the ceiling, but it was painted over on the outside.

"Why do we have a window that we can't see out of?"

"Because it's illegal to house us in a place without a window," John said with authority. I didn't feel satisfied.

"Okay, then why is it painted?" I asked.

"The law doesn't say that the window has to be see through," he replied as he pushed the little round button in the wall to flush the toilet.

My eyebrows formed a question, "So you think it makes perfect sense that they have painted the windows even though it costs more to do that?"

He approached my boat. "Hey if you had built an empire based on marketing the idea that your enemies are some really bad people, and you imprisoned them, then you'd do everything you could to keep people convinced that the people you have are really bad people. And the way it works is, the more they fuck with us, the more people are convinced that we deserve it. And the more people can't see us the more they get away with thinking we are animals that need to be put down."

He began scratching his neck.

"You see," he said, "this is another example of how they know how to play the game. You and me, we broke the law and got caught. But they... no they don't get caught, because while they are off doing one thing with this hand, on the other hand they get real creative—finding ways to break the point of the law without actually breaking the law. That's why they keep getting away with murder. Cuz they always leave something for you to find if you look, something that justifies you looking but ultimately you can't get them for."

He sat down on my boat and then pointed to the floor near our feet and said, "Besides, look, we lucked out. You see this?"

There was a spot of light coming through a small hole in the frosted paint from the upper part of the window.

"So?" I said.

"So, rocket scientist, if you get up on your tiptoes you might be able to see out that hole. There's alligators or some shit down there. I haven't seen them myself because I'm too short, but that's what they say."

For the next hour I tried to contort my body to see out the hole as John kept asking me what I saw.

Meanwhile, the cellmate that slept beneath Toenails started washing his clothing—in the toilet. Sitting on the floor, straddling the toilet between his legs, wearing nothing but his white boxers and his plastic slippers, he thoroughly scrubbed his bar of soap into his jumpsuit and then began splashing and slurping it in the toilet bowl. Then he wrung it out, flushed the toilet to get fresh water, and repeated the entire process.

I took a break from twisting my neck to get my eye in the right spot. Looking down at this makeshift laundromat I said faintly, "I will never do that."

"We'll see," he said in response without missing a beat. I was surprised he had heard me. "I said the same thing, but feel free to try and hold out, ain't nothin' to me."

"Jamal's right," John said. "You got to adapt to the jungle you live in or you'll never survive." I ignored them both and continued looking out the little hole in the window. Jamal kept sloshing his clothes in the toilet, flushing, and repeating.

"Evidently baby alligators don't mind that big mess of razor wire because there are two of them just hanging out under it," I said a couple of minutes later. By the time the Sun went down one of the alligators had moved a couple of feet, but the other hadn't moved at all.

At ten 'o clock the officer yelled, "lights out!" He turned all the lights off from his control panel, and then, to my surprise, the pod got quiet. I laid back and tried to forget about the guy who wants to get away with murder, the toilet laundromat, and the longest and dirtiest toenails I had ever seen.

...

I woke to a loud series of popping sounds migrating through the pod as the doors electronically opened. An electronic buzzing lingered for a couple of seconds in each lock after the door latched fully clicked.

"Chow time, chow time, chow time!" the officer yelled. A cart had been wheeled to the main door of the pod. I followed my cellmates down the stairs and got in line. The food cart consisted of dark brown plastic trays, stacked on top of each other. Each of us had to take whatever tray was on top when we reached the cart. My tray had sloppy goop dripping down one side of it. I walked between tables to find an empty seat. Black men on both sides of me complained.

"Hey man!" one said as I passed by him. He put his hands over his tray.

"Muthafucka learn some respek," another said as he leaned forward putting his upper body directly over his food.

I sat down next to a white man in his forties and asked, "What was that all about?"

"What?" he responded, still half asleep.

"Those guys freaking out," I said.

"Oh," he said with plain white grits still in his mouth. "They don't like it if anyone is within reach of them when they have food."

"Seriously?" I asked.

He raised his eyebrows, tilted his head and then returned to eating.

We returned to our cells, the doors closed behind, and the day continued. The large muscular black man that slept beneath John, who they called Cue Ball, got up and sat on the toilet with his clothes still on. His head was abnormally large, round, and completely bald. He began to bounce up and down on the toilet over and over. I looked at John and said, "What's he..." John quickly shook his head and signaled for me not to say anything and remain quiet. He got out of bed and casually walked to the bars, watching the officer outside, but pretending not to be watching him.

John started a conversation to distract anyone that might be listening to the bouncing. "Hey Cue Ball," he said, "why don't we see if the rocket scientist here can guess how you got your name?"

"Well it ain't because of my shiny white head," Cue Ball said with a smirk. His voice was much deeper than I expected, suggesting that he might have been trying to sound intimidating, but the way he was bouncing up and down really undermined that effort. They both looked at me like they were waiting for me to guess.

"Yeah, that's exactly the kind of thing that college prepared me for," I said sarcastically.

"Come on, it will be fun," John said. I didn't reply.

John moved his face in front of mine from Cue Ball's point of view and began guessing as if he was speaking for me, changing his voice to sarcastically mimic me. "Cuz you look the same from every side? Oh, I know, because your momma got pregnant from stuffing a cue ball up her twat after an ape came on it?" He was moving around a bit now, almost as if he was in a boxing ring. ""Cause before yo daddy left yo momma he smacked you upside your head with a cue ball." Cue Ball looked at him and stopped bouncing.

"No, no, no, wait, I got it, because your balls…"

"Cuz when I play the game I'm the last muthafucka standing," Cue Ball said cutting him off. I couldn't tell if he was being serious or not.

John smirked slightly and said, "Don't mean a thing if you's always the one picking the game. Know what I'm talking about?"

Cue Ball ignored John and continued to bounce on the toilet for over a minute. John lost interest and returned to looking through the bars across the pod. Cue Ball looked inside the bowl and was obviously satisfied. He got off the pot, took off one of his socks, and then dipped it inside. Next he pulled out the wet sock and wrung it out into the sink. Over and over he continued to remove all the water until there was a faint sucking sound coming from the toilet.

At this point Cue Ball grabbed a comb from under his mattress and attached it to a six-foot piece of floss. Then he reached into the toilet and pushed the comb into the pipes while keeping hold of the end of the string with his other hand. For a minute or so he fished the bowl, letting the string drop down the pipes then jerking it back. Then, to my surprise, he pulled up a plastic bag tied to another string. The bag contained a lighter and some hand rolled cigarettes.

Jamal and Toenails had been completely unresponsive during this entire process. I had thought that Toenails was asleep the entire time, but as soon as Cue Ball pulled up that plastic bag they both got out of their bunks. In seconds, all four of them were kneeling around the toilet with their faces close enough to lick it. Apparently, I had become the default look out.

One by one they lit up, taking smoke as deep into their lungs as they could, then leaning over the toilet bowl like they were going to puke and very carefully blowing their smoke into it. This procedure was surprisingly effective. There was no lingering smell of smoke at all.

When they were done, Cue Ball rewrapped his treasures back inside the plastic bag they came from and stuffed it all back inside the sewer pipes. Then they all brushed their teeth with their issued stubby toothbrushes and mini tubes of toothpaste.

When it was all over, I noticed that Jamal was walking with a serious limp as he paced around the cell.

"You okay?" I asked.

"What ya mean?" Jamal replied.

"Is your leg okay?" I said pointing to his limping leg.

He shot me a withering look that confused me.

"I'm sure you could put in a cop out and try to go to medical to check it out," I added.

192

He raised his hands high and shook them as he spoke. "Fuck you man, dis my pimp walk. Took me foe yee-ohs to massa dis."

```
卌 卌 卌 卌 卌 卌 卌 卌 卌 卌 卌 卌 卌 卌
卌 卌 卌 卌 卌 卌 卌 卌 卌 卌 卌 卌 卌 卌
卌 卌 卌 卌 卌 卌 卌 卌 卌 卌 卌 卌 卌 卌
卌 卌 卌 卌 卌 卌 卌 卌 卌 卌 卌 卌 卌 卌
卌 卌 卌 卌
卌 卌 |
```

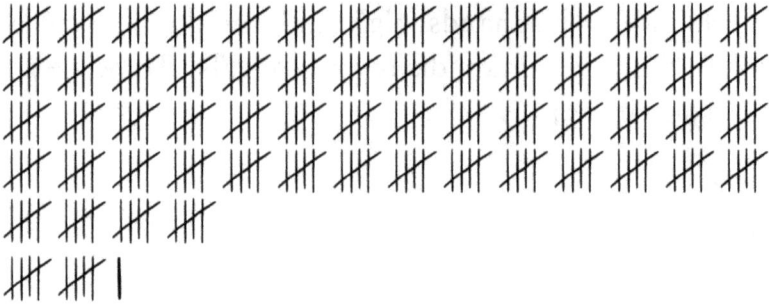

During the middle of the day the officers usually popped our cell doors to let us roam around the pod for a few hours. For better or worse, this enabled us all to get to become more acquainted with the other characters in the pod.

The toughest and loudest man in the room went by the name "Dread". He was a tall black man with dread locks down to his mid back and a full dark beard. His skin was just a little darker than mine, but he easily had double my muscle mass. Dread was heavily interested in promoting his alpha male status. He walked with his shoulders back, posturing, testing the waters with each new person. The people that he found particularly weak got a personal invite/order to participate in his Bible study group. Every day he read the Bible to them for an hour, loudly emphasizing nearly every other word, like he was reading it for the first time, but wanting everyone else to think he was an authority.

Open pod time became my time to walk. I quickly made a routine out of the greatest loop available. Up the stairs on the left, on the second-floor balcony, past the showers, down the stairs on the right, under the stairs, then around the outskirt of the main room.

Rinse, repeat.

Some people stayed in their cells and tried to nap during this time, some went to hang out with people from different cells. A large group of people watched TV. The tables furthest from the pod officer usually became occupied with culturally paired groups of four, playing slap 'em down Dominos, or card games like Spades and Hearts. Making my way around my selected track, I heard men breathing heavy as they engaged in routine push-ups, sit-ups, and leg exercises in their cells. Two cells were particularly popular. They both belonged to orderlies, who had access to large plastic bags that could be filled with water and used as weights.

From every corner of the pod I could hear the Bible study session. "And GOD... CAST dem OUT."

Returning to my cell I found Jamal lying on his bed. I reached down and grabbed my sheet. He understood this motion and promptly exited the cell. I tied the sheet to the bars, making the room mostly private. Then I pulled my orange jumpsuit and my boxers down past my knees. It was difficult to relax. The sheet didn't block out any of the sound.

"Yo dawg, dat's my cousin! Dat's my cousin." Obviously, someone below was watching either COPS or Jerry Springer on the television.

"Come on," I told myself as I tried to concentrate, desperate for relief from this hell. "Escape here for just one minute today."

"But I suffer not a WOMAN to TEACH, nor to

usurp AUTHORITY over the MAN, but to BE in SILENCE."

"Awwww booooyeeeee," another said as he slammed down a domino loudly on the metal table. "What you gonna do now? That's right, that's right, that's what I'm talk'n bout."

When I was finished I pushed the little round metal button in the wall, washed my hands, and took the sheet down.

I went downstairs and started doing push-ups in a relatively empty spot. A creepy white guy who lived in the cell below mine 'posted up' near me. Several times on the way to chow he had made it known that he was blind as he stumbled his way around. So I didn't think much of the fact that he was standing next to one of the cement pillars with his eyes locked on something of no particular interest.

Between sets I stood up and glanced his way. Now he was looking down, had both hands in his pants and appeared to be tying something to his penis. When he was done he shook his leg for a bit, bent over and grabbed a string that had passed all the way down to his foot.

After my next set, I stood up and saw him causally leaning against the pillar still looking past me towards the main pod door. As I went down for my third set of push-ups I heard, "Pill call!"

People began to line up for their medicine. Standing back up, I noticed that the blind guy was now tapping his foot relentlessly.

The nurse was a plain, yet attractive, lady in her forties with short curly hair. He was staring her down, trying to get creative with his imagined violations of consent, and going to town with his tap dance.

"Hey! Hey man!" he said as he swatted his hand sideways gesturing for me to move out of his line of sight. I stood there bewildered.

He continued, "Hey man, hey man, have some respeck."

"Respect?" I snapped back. He kept motioning for me to move.

People started watching, sensing that a fight might ensue. I started to walk away, but then swung around closer to him. "What happened to you being blind?" I asked.

"Do your own time man," he quipped as he leaned to the side to see around me, still tapping his foot.

• • •

Several days later, as we returned to our cells for lock down, I checked the windowsill as the last cellmate in latched the door closed behind him.

"I think mine are ready," I said to John. "Check yours." He joined me as we picked up little squares that we had crafted out of toilet paper and toothpaste. We both sat back down on the boat and began wrapping our hardened squares with floss and bits of string that had been carefully pulled from the stuffing in our mattresses.

"You have to make it as tight as possible, without cutting into the cube," I said. After wrapping the cubes several times, we added a dab of toothpaste to fix it all in place. We started mixing more material to add to our squares. When we were done we squished the new outer layers with our fingers until they were as square as possible and placed them back in the windowsill to dry. Soon, we had makeshift dice; little cubes of chance in a place where the stench of bad luck was so concentrated it almost cast a shadow.

As the days passed, some prisoners left, and new ones took their place. Dread was gaining followers. Now he had sixteen people regularly attending his Christian services, but he was still the only one talking in them.

We were now playing dice games, inventing new rules as we went.

"Laundry!" an officer yelled. We scooped up our dice and hid them deftly under my boat. The cart slowly made its rounds. An officer circled with a clipboard as an orderly from another pod stayed with the cart on the ground floor. When the officer came to our cell we stripped to our boxers and stood in line.

First in line, I pushed my jumpsuit between the bars and said, "Double X." The officer took my outfit and tossed it over the railing behind him into the bin.

"You'll take a Large," the officer said as he made a mark on his clipboard.

"No, that was a Double X," I pleaded.

"You'll take a Large," he repeated. He looked over

at the orderly, commanding his obedience. The orderly reached for the pile of folded up outfits marked 'Large' and then threw it up to the officer. The officer handed it to me through the bars.

Everyone else in the cell began putting their outfits back on.

"I'm good boss," one of them said.

"Mine still smells clean," another said.

The officer moved on to the next cell. Jamal began laughing at me as I stood there in my white boxers holding an outfit far too small for me.

Two hours later the pod officer made his rounds and yelled at me.

"Put your clothes all the way on convict. Up over your shoulders!"

I had the jumpsuit down to my waist, wrapping the arms around me like a jacket.

With a voice that begged for leniency I said, "This thing is way too small for me. I can't fit."

"I bet they can find you one that fits better in C-pod," he threatened. I untied the arms and pulled it over my shoulders giving myself a very serious and uncomfortable wedgie.

The officer moved on and all of my cellmates started snickering.

"You'll never wash your clothes in the toilet huh? Suit yourself," Jamal said. They all thought that was pretty clever. I glared at them and went to sit down, but the outfit was too tight for sitting. I stood right back up and they all laughed some more.

"You know what the best part is?" he continued while still laughing. "Now that he has that size, muthafucka's stuck with it."

...

I pulled the jumpsuit over my shoulder just before the officer reached our cell.

"Hey CO, what time is it?" John asked as the officer passed our cell. "Why? You got a date?"

"Yeah, and she's going to be real mad if I'm late, so what time is it?" John added.

"Three fifteen," the officer said as he left. John gave me a head nod.

As the officer walked away I undid the top of my jumpsuit and then slid my boat to the side. Then I took my stubby golf pencil and circled the light spot on the floor and wrote the time and the date next to all the other circles previously marked. Slowly but surely, our captive sundial became a way to mark the passage of time in this warped place.

꜔꜔꜔꜔꜔꜔꜔꜔꜔꜔꜔꜔꜔꜔꜔
꜔꜔꜔꜔꜔꜔꜔꜔꜔꜔꜔꜔꜔꜔꜔
꜔꜔꜔꜔꜔꜔꜔꜔꜔꜔꜔꜔꜔꜔꜔
꜔꜔꜔꜔꜔꜔꜔꜔꜔꜔꜔꜔꜔꜔
꜔꜔꜔꜔꜔꜔꜔꜔꜔꜔꜔꜔||||

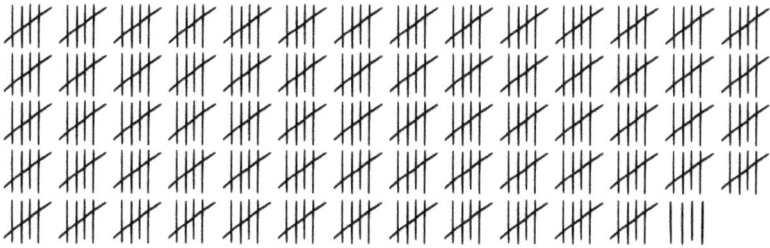

The doors popped open, leaving that two second lingering buzzing sound. I was sitting cross-legged on my boat, playing spider solitaire.

"Rec!" the CO yelled.

Cue Ball got up right away. Toenails didn't move at all. John took a break from piecing together his draft of *How to Get Away with Murder*, and climbed out of his bunk, stepping on Cue Ball's bunk in the process.

"Hey, Hey!" Cue Ball yelled. He came back into the cell furious. "I told you, don't ever put your nasty feet on my muthafuckin' bed."

"I got to get down Cue," John said. "Can't be jumping up and down all the time. How about you fold your mattress out of the way if you don't want me touching it?"

"What did you say?" Cue Ball said moving aggressively towards him.

"I said you can just move your mattress out of the way, if you don't want me to touch it when I climb down."

Cue Ball started breathing faster, moving his head from side to side and leaning in further towards John's face.

"Look Cue, I ain't offering any disrespect here. I

just got to look out for my knees, know what I'm saying?" John's voice was surprisingly absent of fear. He used his posture to stand his ground, but his words were calm.

"All I do in here is go up and down this cage, probably a dozen times a day, surely we can work something out?" Cue Ball backed off a bit and then swung his arms in support of his words. "Then just use this end," he said as he pointed to the foot of his bed.

"We cool, we cool," John said as he nodded neutrally.

I left the cell to go to rec. The officer hadn't unlocked the door yet, so I waited just outside my cell leaning on the railing that overlooked the pod.

"Drop that deuce nigga! We gots to go!" a black man yelled from outside the central cell on the bottom floor. "I ain't playing nigga, I'm ready to run this and I ain't gonna wait for you," he said as he banged on the bars of the cell. The man behind the shit sheet didn't respond.

The impatient man was holding neatly fanned out cards in his hand. With his animated gait he walked back to the stainless steel table where two others were waiting with cards already in their hands and a fourth pile of cards ready to be put in play. They were playing spades, a four-person game.

Just then the darkest skin person I'd ever seen in my life walked past the card table.

"Hey, hey, my nigga, want to get some of this?" the impatient player asked him. The passer by stopped, turned to face his questioner, and then raised his voice and forcefully yelled, "Do I look BLACK to you?" The card player looked directly at him and didn't pursue. "I'm an INDIO," the passerby exclaimed.

The officer unlocked the rec door. John and I and only six others took the opportunity to go out.

"Did you see that?" I asked.

"See what," he responded as we continued walking down the corrugated metal staircase.

"That guy was completely offended that anyone could ever mistake him for being black," I said.

"And?" John asked.

"Well he's literally the darkest skinned person I've ever seen, maybe even the darkest physically possible."

"What's that got to do with anything?" John asked.

"What do you mean? He just got pissed because that guy thought he was black. Don't you find that a little strange?"

John looked at me and asked, "How would you feel if someone thought you were black?"

"Why would anyone think that I'm black?" I asked.

We were in a cement room with a tall ceiling that was entirely sealed with chain-link fencing, open to the hot and humid Florida air. There was a basketball hoop and two basketballs in the room. The first two men down the stairs kicked off their plastic sandals and immediately began tossing the balls.

John motioned for me to join him by the wall.

"Let me break it down for you, Moon Rock. You ain't the only one that's been to college you know. I've been there too." I looked at him with a bit of surprise.

"Oh yeah, I got my head filled with all them notions that educated people cling to, all that uppity shit that makes them feel they understand a world they don't dare step into. Take 'racism' for example."

One of the basketballs ricocheted right next to us. "Stiff necks like to preach about racism, about how they are above such things, how they would never hate someone just because of their skin color, and feeling all proud of themselves for rising above less evolved sentiments. But the thing is, the racism that they speak of don't exist, never did. It's a figment they made up to make them feel good."

"What are you talking about?" I asked. "Are you seriously saying that there aren't racist people in the world?"

"Listen, Moon Rock, I'm telling you that there aren't people in the world that hate other people just because of their skin color, and pretending that is what racism is about misses the entire point. Race is about identity, it's about a perspective shared among a group, a cultural background, a set of ideas about how to interact, about how to earn prestige, about how you become top shit, about how you get the girl. It's a set of beliefs that shape the identity of one's world. The color of one's hair color, or skin color, has nothing to do with it."

He scrutinized me with his eyes, trying to gauge if I

was following.

"Look," he added, "your ass is rotting away in jail right now, right in the motherfucking heart of where the stiff necks thinks racist people are. Have you seen any of that kind of racism?"

"Of course I have," I declared. "I see it every day."

"No, you don't. Tell me one time that someone in here hated someone else just because of their skin color, or the type of hair they were born with."

"When the new fish come in," I said, "people immediately click up by skin color, shunning people of different color, and supporting people with the same color."

"Is that what you think?" he asked. "Is that what you do?"

"What do you mean?" I asked.

"Do you go out of your way to get along with people with white skin and stay away from those with black skin?"

"No, of course not. I get along with anyone that seems like a decent person."

"Exactly, and the very notion of "decent person" is a reflection of identity, of your values, of what you hold dear. It's a plea for others that share your perspective."

"What's your point?" I asked.

"My point is that outside of your cellies, I've only seen you spend any significant time with only one black skin person in this whole pod. The rest are all white skinned. Is that because of their skin?"

"Of course not," I said.

John paused for a bit and then continued, "You know that kid, downstairs that they call Patch?"

"Yeah."

"Is he white or black?" he asked.

I was about to answer, but John cut me off.

"He has white skin, but he walks around with a pimp walk, he talks loud and proud about slinging his dope, and his bitches, calls himself a nigga, others call him nigga, his vocabulary is practiced and fine-tuned to be indistinguishable from everyone else that calls themselves a nigga, he brags about getting a ten piece, he thinks it's funny to retell stories about how he strung people out on drugs and then when they couldn't find money for more he would make them suck their own shit through a straw, or fuck their wife in the ass for the next hit, and a whole bunch of other fucked up things. Now tell me, what culture does he belong to?"

I didn't answer.

"Yeah, you're starting to see it aren't you? The house of cards is coming down. You're starting to see how the ivory towers are just built as self-serving empires, praising their loftiness, all the while completely ignoring the real issues, all the while contributing to the very momentum of the problems they imagine themselves being beyond."

"And what are the real issues?" I asked.

"Power," he said. For a brief moment his eyes glazed over. He looked away, like he was lost in a memory, and then a few seconds later he continued.

"The real issue," he said, "is what power is and what it could be." There was a slight inflection of pain in his voice. I looked up through the fenced ceiling, seeing only blue sky.

"In a world with more than one person," he said, "someone's always going to be doing something that somebody else don't like, and one motherfucker is always going to have more privilege and power than others. That, my friend, we will never escape. But what," he said as he raised his index finger, "what do those in power do?"

I switched my gaze back and forth between him and the sky above, trying to gauge if this was one of his memorized speeches, or something he was making up on the spot, while watching for a cloud, or a bird, or something to come into view.

"Today," he said as he moved more squarely in front of me, "being in power means that you don't have to give a fuck why others do what they do, or try to understand them at all. Those in power simply punish others for doing what they don't like, but they don't get punished for doing what those without power don't like.

Punishment has become a display of power, a display that they are above being punished. They start wars, but we don't call them tyrants. They murder thousands of people for oil rights, but we don't call them mass murders. They declare new decrees and orders for others to follow, but we don't call them dictators."

His eyes were steely, voice galvanized. "Today those in power show their power by doing the worst things they can think of and getting away with it in broad daylight. Fuck, the more they get away with it, the more they are praised for it. Nowadays we give power to the small minds, the brutes, the loudest voices, because that's what we think power is. We don't value patience, wisdom, or true courage any more. We've been told to want more stuff, that feeling safe is the great prize, and we throw away all of our freedoms and nobility to have it. But feeling safe is a lie. Ain't no way to actually be safe. And all that shit everyone been hoarding hasn't made 'em one bit happier. But no one sees through the lies. So now we give power away to the worst of the worst because all we have left is the lie. We have to pretend, we have to believe, or else we end up waking up one fucking morning realizing the monstrosity of what we have done."

I interjected, "I don't think that…"

He scolded me with his eyes, demanding that I listen until he finished. "Our masters have crafted a clever bullshit story—convincing us that people chose their lives, that each of us could have done otherwise at any point. They've made us believe that whenever we feel something it's because we chose something, and we've been munching on this bullshit for so long we can't see behind that story any more. We've dropped cause and effect for blame and praise, but it doesn't serve us, it serves them. The privileged want everyone to believe that their advantaged position is because of their choices, and that the shit pile life everyone else has is because of their shitty choices. That way they don't have to take the long hard look at reality, and they can keep telling themselves that they are different, better, more deserving. That way they don't have to ask what caused each person to make those choices in the first place."

All the other men outside were now playing HORSE with the basketball.

"Shit, it's pretty obvious that the world is fucked up when the strong proudly cast their judgments and inflict suffering on the world and then get praised for it," he added. "But nobody is saying anything about it. Nobody is doing anything about it. It's as if nobody thinks there's another way."

He kicked off his plastic footwear but kept his attention on me.

"I'm telling you, Moon Rock, it hasn't always been that way, and doesn't need to be that way. There have been those with power who used their privilege for something other than control and dominion. There have been those that saw past the emptiness of that game and reached for something more, became something more, and in so doing, they became a beacon for all of humanity."

"Who?" I asked.

"Their names don't matter," he said. "They didn't do it for fame, or glory, or prestige. They did it for something far greater, something that this world of commercialism and intentional manipulation has long turned away from. They saw past it all and reached nirvana."

Suddenly, he signaled with his head as he said, "Come on." The game of HORSE was ending. He jumped in line for the next one. I stepped out of my plastic shoes and joined in.

卌 卌 卌 卌 卌 卌 卌 卌 卌 卌 卌 卌 卌 卌
卌 卌 卌 卌 卌 卌 卌 卌 卌 卌 卌 卌 卌 卌
卌 卌 卌 卌 卌 卌 卌 卌 卌 卌 卌 卌 卌 卌
卌 卌 卌 卌 卌 卌 卌 卌 卌 卌 卌 卌 卌 卌
卌 卌 卌 卌 卌 卌 卌 卌 卌 卌 卌 卌 卌 卌
卌 卌

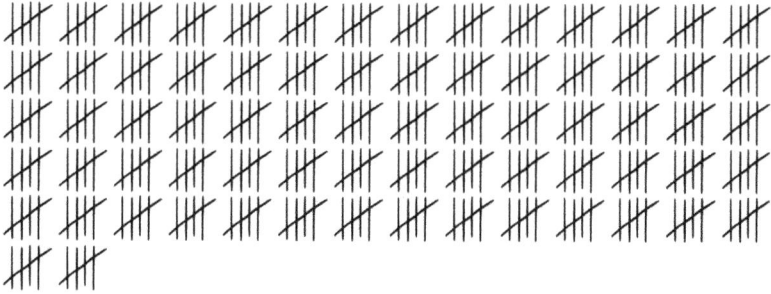

"Lock down!" the pod officer yelled. It was earlier than normal. Toenails was already laying in his bunk, flat on his back with his feet still sticking out over the end of the bed. Cue Ball was the last one in the cell. "Coming or going?" he asked as he latched the door behind him.

"Coming," John said.

"How you know?" Cue Ball asked.

"Cuz this cage is already past capacity," he said as he pointed to me sitting down on my boat. "So they might as well keep shoving more boats in this shit hole." Cue Ball seemed satisfied with this reasoning.

We all watched from our cells to see the only novel event that was going to happen today. Like everything else, it started with a buzzing sound.

The new batch was made up of three sorry scraps. The first was black skinned with long scraggly dreads, dragging in his boat with a pimp walk so practiced that it looked like he needed a hip replacement. The second was also black skinned, in his early thirties, with a shiny head and a huge sagittal crest like a wild dog. The third was white skinned, average height, with a patchy beard and hair down to his shoulders. His eyes were twitchy and the officer had some trouble getting the cuffs off of him because he couldn't sit still.

He acted as if he was seeing ghosts, turning his head and backing away from whatever direction he was looking. He was clearly detoxing and in severe withdrawal. It was so obvious that no one could have missed it, which meant that somewhere along the chain of command, someone decided to make an 'error' on purpose. Perhaps they were looking for a little entertainment at the expense of his abject misery.

The pod officer put them each in different cells. The detoxing man was placed in a corner cell on the bottom floor, right next to Dread's cell.

"Hey newbie," Dread said in a hoarse whisper after things had settled down. "Yeah, you. Hey man, don't let them fuck with you okay?"

"What do you mean?" the suggestible and unstable man said with audible fear in his voice. Dread waited for him to approach the bars.

"Well, in about twenty minutes they're going to send one of their spies, dressed up as the nurse at pill call. But don't you let them fool you man. You gotta be smart."

"Spies for what?" the new guy asked.

"Hey man, I'm trying to help you. You gotta be focused. If they call your name then you'll know I'm right. They're gonna come to that door, call your name, and make you think you's gonna see the nurse, but that's when they's gonna get you."

"They already got me," he said with a wavering

voice.

"Hey man, I'm trying to save your life. If you don't want to live, that's your business. I'm just saying that ain't no one ever gonna to hear from you again if you go see that nurse."

"What? What do you mean?" The man was already freaking out, the paranoia seeping into every twitch of his facial muscles. A few people in the pod started chuckling, thinking that Dread's game was fun. The pod officer was at his desk in the middle of the room, with headphones on, watching a movie on his little screen.

"They say that sometimes they just use 'em for practice, you know, to see how many hits a man can take before he dies, or see how much he can bleed before kicking the can. Other times they lock you up in a room just to watch you go crazy as the years pass, without ever telling you a word. You just disappear and nobody ever knows where you went."

"Hey man, no, I have to get out of here!" the new man said with a trembling voice, the whites of his eyes gleaming.

"Don't worry man, it will be just fine," Dread assured. "You just gotta be smart. Just remember when they pop your door, don't let 'em get you."

He couldn't hold still. He was pacing, sweating and nervous.

"What am I supposed to do?" he asked.

"You see that CO over there?" Dread asked. The officer had his feet kicked up on his desk, reclining in his chair as he watched his show.

"Yeah."

"Well, when they call your name and pop your door, you walk up pretending that you don't know nothing. Then when you get close to his chair you reach over and snap his neck! Quick and hard."

"I don't see how…"

"Hey! Hey man!" Dread interrupted. "You got to pay attention. Look at that guy. He's one of the spies too. He's the reason you are in here in the first place! They are fucking with you man. You gonna let them do that? You gonna let them just kill you and that's that?"

"I don't want to die," the man moaned, starting to cry.

This triggered a few prisoners to laugh even louder.

"You don't have to, but you have to be smarter than them. They don't know that you know about their plan. You have the advantage, but you have to be quick and strong. Can you be quick and strong?"

"I think so," he squeaked out.

"Good. Now practice. Take your hands and imagine grabbing his head and snapping his neck."

The man followed his instructions, acting out the motion desperately over and over, confused, scared and clumsy.

I was standing at the bars in my cell.

"Moon," John whispered, watching me bristle. I ignored him.

"He's just fucking with you, man," I yelled out.

Dread quickly retorted, "Don't listen to them, man,

they all want to see you die. Look at me. I'm your only friend in here. I want you to get through this. You've got to blow the lid on this whole thing and expose them spies. Otherwise they will never let you be."

John jumped down from his bed and grabbed my shoulder. He was shaking his head fervently.

"What?" I asked. "If he tries to kill the CO they will put him away for attempted murder. He's probably here on some drunken disorderly thing and will be out in less than a month and now Dread is trying to really fuck up his life."

"Ain't your business man," John said with a very serious look. The rest of my cellmates were staring at me like I had just killed a cat with a butcher knife in a crazy fit.

"Didn't you tell me that power could be different?" I asked.

"Yeah," John said, "but first you have to be in power." He grabbed the bars to make his point. "Come on," he added as he grabbed his deck of cards.

Ten minutes later, the nurse arrived. The pod officer opened the door for her and she stood behind her cart in the doorway.

I stopped playing the card game, attention focused on the scene.

"Hey," John said drawing my attention. "That ain't the way."

"Jackson!" she yelled. The pod officer pushed a button for the man's cell and popped it open. Then the officer went back to watching his movie.

The newbie grabbed the barred metal door and pulled it back shut.

"I don't want any," he proclaimed with a cracking voice.

She yelled out again, "Inmate Jackson... Inmate Jackson."

The pod officer heard her yelling and then pushed the button again, buzzing it a few times in a row. The door popped back open.

Jackson slowly and timidly came out of his cell.

"Be strong man. Outsmart them. Fast and quick," Dread encouraged in a hushed voice.

He exited his cell slowly. Then he walked the line between his cell and the nurse. He approached slow at first, but gradually went faster and faster. The pod officer was still in his chair, with his feet up on the desk.

Jackson passed the officer, looked at the nurse and then quickly turned back. He rushed over to the officer, grabbed his head with both hands and twisted as hard and fast as he could.

The officer spun around and fell on the ground. He began screaming and immediately hit his red panic button on his hand radio. The nurse was also talking on her radio, "Code Red, A-Pod, Code Red, A-Pod." The swivel chair had just saved the officer's life.

Jackson panicked. At first he just stood there looking around like he had no idea what was happening, wondering why he was even there. Then it became clear that he realized everything was pointing towards him, and with a look of frantic confusion he fled up the stairs, past my cell.

"Just get down on the floor," I yelled at him. "You have to lay down on your belly and put your hands behind your head." The pod was full of reverberating sounds. Some were laughing, others were yelling at the man on the run, giving him conflicting commands.

Twenty officers came rushing in, with full armored outfits, zaping sticks, shocking shields, face guards, and complete combat gear.

"They're both spies," Jackson yelled to the combat squad, pointing at the officer and the nurse. "You have to get them," he said.

To his surprise they ignored his advice. They split into two groups rushing up both sets of stairs. Near the corner of the balcony, next to the showers, we all watched as the black-clad troopers closed in on Jackson.

He began screaming, "I'm not supposed to be here. This isn't real." He became more and more jumpy, second-guessing every step he took.

"Leave me alone. Leave me alone," he pleaded.

As they approached, he scaled the railing so that he could jump off the balcony.

"Better to kill yourself than let them get you," one of the voices behind bars encouraged.

The lead officers halted and those playing the caboose of this pain train rushed back down the stairs to get beneath him.

"Get down and put your hands on your head,"

another inmate suggested. "That's the only way you're going to survive this."

Some of the officers were right in front of my cell.

"Go easy on him, he's not all there," I pleaded.

"We don't go easy on cop killers," they replied with vicious conviction.

Jackson was half way up the railing but didn't jump. When it was clear that he was too afraid to make the leap, officers rushed him, threw him on the ground and started breaking in their brand new batons.

"Stop, stop, owww, please stop." They kept hitting him until the pleas stopped, then dragged him out of the pod by his twitchy limbs.

"They're spies," he faintly repeated. Then he suddenly went still and silent, even as two others grabbed him to carry him down the stairs.

...

The next morning, walking down the stairs to stand in line for the breakfast tray felt different. The place was strangely void of chatter and nearly all of the prisoners were looking at their feet and keeping to themselves more than usual. I sat down at an empty table and began to eat my grits. Before acquiring his tray, Dread approached me, put one foot up on the chair next to me and loudly proclaimed himself king of the violent snarl-toothed gorillas with his body language.

"You know," he said. "There's doing time, and

then there's doing hard time. Them's that don't know how to mind their own business end up doing hard time, know what I'm talkn' bout, know I mean?"

I stopped eating my grits and replied, "What kind of time do you think Jackson is going to do now?"

He squinted his eyes and leaned in, the threat was unmistakable. "You think you're better than me, Moon Rock? You think you should be the one making decisions around here?"

He took a step back and rose to full height. The pod officer clearly took notice of him. I remained sitting, with my outfit wedged up my ass, and looked back at my tray. Then I turned my head and issued in a low tone, "I was just asking you a question. I've got a few more questions if you want to hear them." He breathed heavy, nostrils flaring as he glanced at the officer. Then he leaned towards me, slowly menacing.

"Someone's going to be teaching you your place real soon, Moon Rock, you can count on that. God doesn't stand for such arrogance."

He got up to get his tray. "Real soon."

He joined the food line right as the second to last person grabbed their tray.

"Hey! Did you just touch my tray?" Dread yelled at the scrawny, quiet white kid in front of him whom people called Worm. There was only one tray left on the cart.

"What?" the Kid said timidly.

"You just touched my tray," Dread reasserted.

"No, no, I don't know what you're talking about."

Dread stepped into the Kid's space, fully intimidating as he closed the distance between them. Worm didn't know what to do.

"You touched my tray. Muthafucka touched my tray!" Dread declared again.

Confused and half-asleep, Worm stood there with quickened breath... and then snapped. Using both hands, he swung his tray at Dread's head, hitting him square in the jaw. Messy goo splashed all over Dread's face, sticking in his hair and dripping down his clothes. Dread reached down and grabbed Worm, twisting the front of his clothes in his fist. He slowly raised his other hand, preparing to hit him and making a big show of it, but before he went through with it the officer stood up blew his whistle and yelled, "Lock Down!"

Worm was cringing, waiting to be hit. Dread looked over at the officer, loosened his grip, and then shoved Worm away from him. The officer yelled again, "Lock down! Lock down!" The shrill whistle continued.

Everyone got up, shoveling the rest of their food in their mouths as fast as they could before they dropped off their trays and returned to their cells.

. . .

Nearly thirty minutes later, the officer opened the pod door and went out into the hallway for his routine coffee refill. As soon as he was gone, Dread yelled across the pod. "Hey Worm! When they pop open these doors I'm going to end your bit."

He started shadow boxing in his cell, punching the air and dancing on his feet, making a big show of his intentions.

"You hear me Worm?" he yelled. "Today is your last day muthafucka. The end of your bit!"

The officer came back in the pod and closed the door. Dread kept shadow boxing, making breathing sounds, "Tsss, Tsss, whooo."

At shift change, the pod door opened again and the new duty officer entered. The officer finishing his shift grabbed his bag from beneath his desk, gave a quick nod to the officer replacing him, and exited the pod without saying a word about the tense situation. Dread was still shadow boxing, making obvious sounds that echoed through the pod.

As soon as the pod door was closed behind him, the new officer popped open all of the cells and yelled "Pod time".

Everyone on the top floor came out of their cells and stood on the balcony to watch. Most prisoners on the bottom floor stayed in their cells, standing where they could see from inside their bars, or in their doorways. To my surprise Worm came out of his cell immediately. He didn't even try to lock himself back in his cell. Dread came out dancing and punching the air, but moving forward very slowly.

"Come on," Worm said. There was no hesitation in his eyes.

The officer noticed what was going on right away

and blew his whistle and yelled, "Lock down." Nobody moved.

Dread started making his was across the pod, but then to everyone's surprise Worm kicked off his plastic flip-flops and quickly tore off his clothes–all of his clothes. He just stood there completely naked waiting for Dread to make a move.

Dread stood there frozen. Twenty long seconds went by in near silence. It was a naked stunned stand-off. Officers rushed in. Everyone except the two combatants went back into their cells. The officers positioned themselves between the would-be fighters.

"Put your clothes on," one of the officers ordered. Worm slowly picked up his clothes. As soon as he finished dressing the officers escorted both of them out of the pod.

"This ain't over," Dread yelled at Worm in an attempt to save face, just before he was pushed out of the door.

"Nice to see something got you out of bed," John said to Toenails as we all settled back in our cell.

"Fuck you man," Toenails replied.

"If things ever pop off around here, you should be the first one to throw down," John taunted. "Show 'em how nasty likes to slice and dice, kill 'em with a staff infection or some shit, like a T-rex, right?"

"T-rex?" Toenails said.

"It's a metaphor, you potato with eyes," John replied.

"Eat shit punk," Toenails retorted.

"Big words for you," John said. "I'm proud of you."

After all of the commotion died down I asked John, "Why didn't Dread fight him after all that talk?"

"Are you kidding?" he chuckled. "You'd never live down punching a naked dude!" My cellmates, including Toenails, started laughing.

```
卌 卌 卌 卌 卌 卌 卌 卌 卌 卌 卌 卌 卌 卌
卌 卌 卌 卌 卌 卌 卌 卌 卌 卌 卌 卌 卌 卌
卌 卌 卌 卌 卌 卌 卌 卌 卌 卌 卌 卌 卌 卌
卌 卌 卌 卌 卌 卌 卌 卌 卌 卌 卌 卌 卌 卌
卌 卌 卌 卌 卌 卌 卌 卌 卌 卌 卌 卌 卌 卌
卌 卌 卌 |||
```

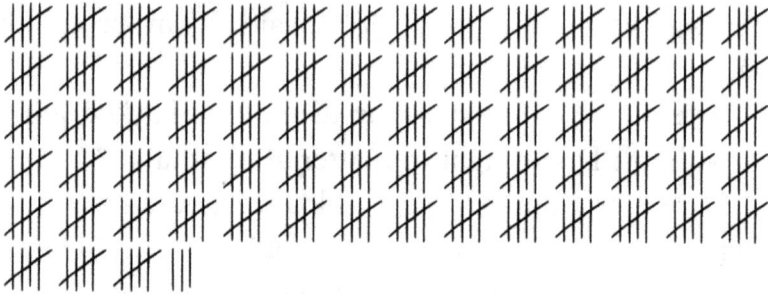

"Six... seven," John blurted out as he finished his round of pushups. I already had my next card flipped over. As soon as he got up I went down and started my set using his same towel for my hands. I counted out loud.

Toenails was watching us from his bunk. "How many push-ups would it be if you did one hundred then ninety-nine, and ninety-eight all the way down?" he asked.

""Five thousand and fifty," I said as I finished my set. Toenails smirked.

"Seriously," I said.

"How could you know that?" he asked. "Nobody can add that many numbers in their head."

"Actually, it's really simple," I said. "In fact, the first person to figure it out was an eight-year-old kid named Carl Freidrich Gauss."

"Uh huh. And I'm s'posed to believe dat?" Toenails asked.

I ignored him and continued. "If I remember right, his teacher punished him for something in the classroom, made him face the chalkboard, and add the first five hundred numbers or something like that. He just wrote down the answer. She didn't believe him so she worked it out clean through the night only to discover that he was right. He went on to be one of the greatest mathematicians of all time."

John signaled for me to do my next set.

"Well it might be easy for great math guru, but I ain't no math genius," Toenails said.

"Can you tell me what one hundred plus one is?" I asked between reps.

Toenails looked at me like I was teasing him.

I finished my set and stood back up. "Well?" I asked.

"Every idiot know dat," Toenails said.

John turned over a face card. "How about fifty times a hundred?" I asked.

John shot out, "five thousand," as he went down. Toenails nodded in agreement.

"Well then," I said. "Guess you're a math genius." Toenails was skeptical.

"Look, all you have to do," I instructed, "is imagine the set of consecutive numbers you want to add up lined up in a row starting from the smallest one on the left and ending with the largest one on the right. Now imagine taking the first and last number and adding them together like you already did. One plus one hundred is a hundred and one. Now set that aside and look at the numbers left. Now add the smallest and biggest numbers left again. What do you get?"

"Two... and ninety-nine... a hundred and one again," Toenails said proudly.

"Exactly. Now if you continue, you just keep getting a hundred and one every time. So... you end up with fifty of those hundred and ones. Which means your answer is just fifty times one hundred and one."

"So..." John added. "This means that you can do this with any length of numbers?"

"Yes," I said.

"What about a thousand?" he asked.

"Same thing, you just take one and a thousand to make a thousand and one and you do it five hundred times, so its five hundred times a thousand and one, or five hundred thousand and five hundred."

"Those kind of tricks are black magic," Jamal said. "They're of the devil."

"It's not a trick," I said. "Look I can teach you." Jamal looked completely uninterested.

"Okay," I said, looking back at Toenails. "Want to know some other cool math stuff? Like what's five thousand two hundred and seventy-one times eleven?"

Toenails gave me the 'what the fuck' look, and John's face widened with interest.

"It's five-seven-nine-eight-one," I said.

"How the fuck do I know if you're right?" Toenails asked. "You could just be making this shit up. We ain't math geniuses with fancy computers and shit in here."

"Well the only difference between being a math genius and not being one is knowing the rules." I replied. "Let me show you the rules."

"I'm good," Toenails said as he started to climb

back up to his upper suite. John chuckled with amusement at my efforts.

"What you got something better to do right now?" I asked.

"Yup, staring at the ceiling," Toenails said with contempt.

"You know," I added, "There was this time I was doing physics homework in a group, and one of the girls in the group was super hot, fit, long hair, beautiful face, with those kind of glasses that really makes you want to know what she's thinking." He was still ignoring me.

"Well she didn't talk very much and we all had calculators right there on the desk as we were working on a problem, but she just spoke out loud, almost as if talking to herself, "what's one hundred and fifteen times eleven?" and I immediately said "one-two-six-five," and then she looked at me with interest."

"Did you fuck her?" Toenails asked.

"Come on man, what kind of question is that?" I said.

"What do you mean what kind of question is that?" John butted in. "It's a very clear one, did–you–fuck–her? Simple question."

They were both fixating on me like I was a social worker about to hand them their welfare checks. Cue Ball was on his bunk slapping his leg, imagining a beat with his eyes closed and nodding his head up and down. I sighed, wondering if I should just let myself drown in this place of polished futility. Then I locked eyes with them and asked, "Do you want to learn how to do this or not?"

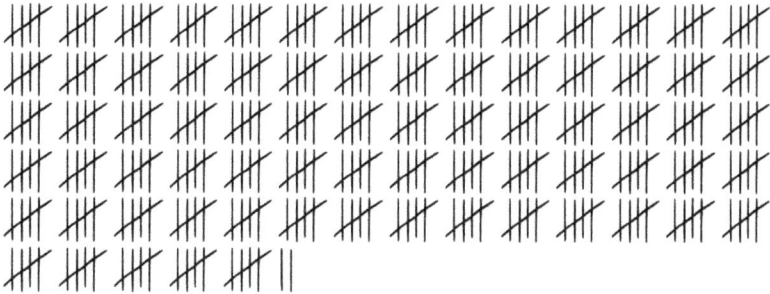

"Maguire, Martinez, Sanchez, Smith, White, roll up your shit!" the officer yelled.

Jamal got up out of bed and rolled his sheet, blanket and towel up in his mattress and placed them by the door.

"Hey Jamal," I said. "Could you trade jumpsuits with me?"

"Tsssss, what? Hell naw," he said as if I had asked him to thank his judge for exercising his judicial license to be racist.

"Come on man, this thing is way too tight on me, and you get to dress out right down there. You'll only have to wear it for five minutes. Come on, please."

He continued to just stand there, waiting for the door to be popped open, itching to leave and never look back.

Several minutes went by as the officer prepared to move the prisoners. When the doors started to pop open Jamal got a bit antsy and then changed his mind. "Fuck me! Come on man, make dis quick."

I stood up right away. "Thanks man. Thanks a lot," I said as I quickly undressed.

We traded outfits, but Jamal didn't pull the

jumpsuit over his shoulders.

He picked up his bedroll and asked, "What time does your calendar say, Moon Rock?"

I moved the boat over and checked to see where the light spot hit the ground as he exited the cell.

"It's five minutes before eleven," I said.

"Peace," Jamal said to the whole room as he trotted down the stairs with an intentional limp for the last time.

Toenails moved his bedroll down to the newly open bottom bunk. He had the seniority. I spent the next hour straddling the toilet, scrubbing my new outfit with soap, and massaging it in the bowl.

"New recruits," someone in the pod yelled. The pod door opened and five new faces joined our tribe. A young white skinned guy, with short brown hair and only one tooth came into our cell.

He looked over at me. "Go ahead man. I'm staying on the boat," I said.

He threw his roll on the empty bunk and began making his bed. He seemed a bit edgy.

"You guys smoke?" he said.

"We've been out for a while now," John said.

"But you got a lighter? I need a lighter."

I watched the pod officer as Cue Ball began bouncing on the toilet.

"Wait, wait," the single-toothed man said. "Let me use it first."

He pulled down his jumpsuit and sat down. We all went to our bunks and waited facing away, but he wasn't looking for privacy. It was almost as if he was trying to make more sounds than necessary. When he was done he reached into the toilet and pulled out a balloon filled with tobacco. It really stunk.

"You guys got papers?" he asked.

"We use these," John said as he pulled out the Bible. After Cue Ball finished fishing for the lighter in the toilet, they all sat around the toilet rolling their tobacco. The smell was getting stronger and stronger.

"What the fuck man?" Toenails said as he squinted his whole face in an attempt to close his nostrils.

"It must have soaked through," the new guy said. "You don't have to have any."

Toenails looked at him for a moment, contorting his face from side to side as if he was trying to decide what kind of bug this was. "What the fuck is up with your mouth?" he said.

"What this?" the new guy said pointing to his only tooth. "This is old chomper, really good for opening up beer cans and such, know what I'm saying?" He smiled with his one tooth smile and then asked Toenails, "What the fuck is up with your feet?"

Toenails wiggled his toes letting the spiraled springs jiggle, which he thought was funny. We all looked away in disgust, except John.

"I'm going to cut those motherfuckers off in your sleep, you nasty fuck. And if they touch me in the process I'm going to cut your feet off with them."

"Dis is natural," Toenails retorted.

"So is cutting off your feet. It's a natural defense

mechanism," John replied, already hacking him up in his mind.

They continued to roll. The entire upper floor of the pod was starting to fill with eye-watering stench. The officer hadn't noticed anything yet, but people in the nearby cells had.

"Agua, agua," several of them began saying. They thought someone was taking a poisonous dump and wanted them to flush midway through their reign on the throne.

I watched as they lit up, taking turns blowing into the toilet. I tried to stay quiet, but started laughing through my T-shirt, pulled up over my nose. They looked at me with dismissive glances.

In a deflated, nose-pinched voice I said, "You know you're addicted when..."

In perfect unison they replied, "Fuck you man," as they continued to light up and pass the ass juice around.

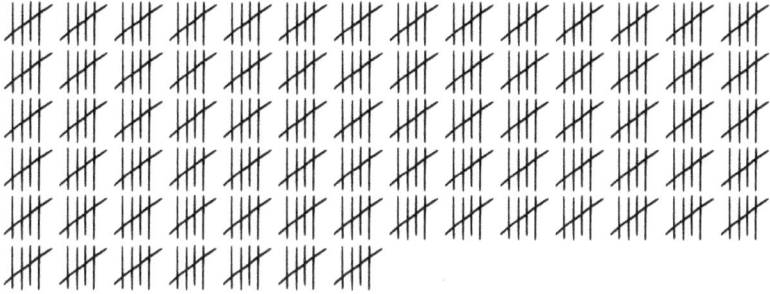

Still breathing heavy from my exercise routine, I went back up the stairs and into my cell and quickly stripped down to my white boxers. I retrieved my small bar of soap and see-through white towel. Chomper was asleep, Toenails was lying on his bunk with his eyes wide open, trying to imagine what his next 'baby's momma' was going to look like.

I shuffled over to the shower, taking one last look at the pod officer below, who seemed consistently uninterested in the showers. I swung the door closed, and threw my towel over it, quickly followed by my boxers. The shower was about six feet deep, with the showerhead at the far end, but the door only covered from the knees to the chest when standing right behind it. Back in the running water, the pod officer could see everything.

I walked to the back of the shower and pushed the little button, pretending to get wet. Ten seconds later the water turned itself off. Back by the door I pretended to soap up, stroking my cock furiously with my eyes closed, aiming for efficiency but also trying to block out reality enough to enjoy myself.

After I finished, I stood tall and quickly glanced

out. The officer still wasn't paying attention. I took a deep breath and relaxed as I exhaled. Now it was much easier to focus.

The water wasn't warm, but it wasn't super cold either. I scrubbed the soap on myself sparingly, trying to conserve it, and rubbed it in as much as possible to maximize how much grease it actually removed. Then I rinsed off, having to re-push the button every ten seconds until I was done.

Gliding my hands firmly along my body, I removed as much water as I could before using the thin towel. After the toweling, I put my boxers back on and then exited the saloon shower.

I dressed methodically in my cell and slowly walked around the open pod. Something drew me towards a kid everyone called "Peter Parker", sitting by himself on the smooth cement with his knees tucked up to his chest. I sat down next to him. He was a very quiet kid, skinny, with brown hair and blue eyes.

"I heard you got sentenced," I said.

Peter didn't say anything. He didn't even turn his head to look at me. His back was against the wall and his face suggested he was falling into the abyss.

"How much time did they give you?" I asked gently.

Peter didn't move. I joined his gaze and sat in silence with him, just sharing the moment.

After several minutes, still looking forward, he broke our quiet trance.

"Who's your judge?" he asked almost whispering.

"Conway," I said.

"I'm sorry," he said, "I've heard she's pretty tough."

"That's what I hear too," I said. "I used to have McCoun. I hear he is fair."

"What happened?" he asked in a sort of detached way.

"They just switched my judge to Conway," I said.

"That's illegal," he said. "They can't switch judges unless the judge dies or they can prove a conflict of interest."

"I've heard, but there's little I can do about it," I said.

He glanced at me and said, "Watch out, if they are pulling moves like that, all that whispering shit never ends up good for you."

"What do you mean?" I asked.

"They switched your judge for a reason," he said. "And if you already had a reasonable judge, then that reason can't be a good one."

"At least I don't have Kovachevich," I said, trying to feel a little better. "I heard she is the worst." I turned my body to face him a little and said, "I read a newspaper article about how she just gave out her millionth year. A million years of suffering that she handed out like candy and they said she is celebrating it."

"Kovachevich," he said, squinting his eyes at the sound of her name and redirecting his gaze back to his original spot.

"Oh, I'm sorry," I said. "I didn't mean... Is that who you had?"

He nodded, full of frustration and anger. After a short pause he began to speak.

"She glared at me with those empty eyes, like I was a chomo or something."

He pulled his hair out of frustration. "She didn't know a thing about me," he continued. "Nothing that mattered. Nothing that was real. She just bought into them stories the prosecutor was making up, bullshit lies, twisting everything into something bad. My whole family was there, everyone that actually knew me but she wasn't interested."

He paused for a moment, swallowed hard, and then continued. "When it was time for sentencing she asked me to stand up. I stood up, with my chains on and this stupid jumpsuit." He looked at his hands, as if he was reliving the moment.

"She told me to walk to the window, so I did" he added. I could feel the tension in his voice.

"When I got to the window she asked me how many birds I saw out there. So I looked around and counted the birds and then I told her. Twelve." She whacked that hammer thing on her desk and said 'okay twelve years.' "

Tears were welling up in his eyes. I didn't know what to say. There was nothing I could do to help.

He wiped the tears from his eyes with the back of his hands and then turned and looked at me.

"I could have said two birds. Why didn't I say two

birds?" he said, voice thin and pained.

I caught his gaze for a moment, seeing my own looking back at me. He was trembling. The world he had believed in had been replaced by the bitter cold of reality, where chaos and meaninglessness reigned and the only real seat of power left was one of puritanical hate.

In silent camaraderie, we sat next to each other until the next lock down, as shards of shattered illusions tore up our insides. The dark abyss, softened by the company of a stranger.

卌 卌 卌 卌 卌 卌 卌 卌 卌 卌 卌 卌 卌 卌
卌 卌 卌 卌 卌 卌 卌 卌 卌 卌 卌 卌 卌 卌
卌 卌 卌 卌 卌 卌 卌 卌 卌 卌 卌 卌 卌 卌
卌 卌 卌 卌 卌 卌 卌 卌 卌 卌 卌 卌 卌 卌
卌 卌 卌 卌 卌 卌 卌 卌 卌 卌 卌 卌 卌 卌
卌 卌 卌 卌 卌 卌 卌 卌 卌 卌

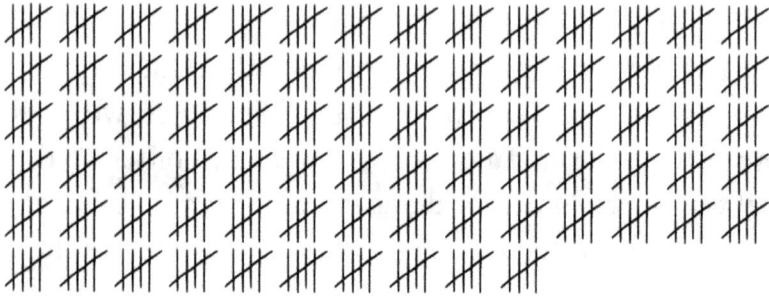

"So? Is that it?" John asked, leaning over my shoulder to read my mail.

" 'Bout time she done wrote you," Toenails said.

"It's a letter from the Mormon Church," I said to both of them as I continued to read it.

John's excitement waned. "I thought you said you weren't Mormon anymore," he intoned.

"Shit, you can't stop being what you was born into," Toenails proclaimed.

"I did," I said to John. "And I'm not Mormon," I said, directing my words at Toenails.

"So what's it say?" John asked.

"It says they are excommunicating me," I said.

Toenails began to laugh. "If they expect to come up in here to cut your dick dey is stupid, man!"

John and I both looked at him with the same profoundly unimpressed expression.

"Excommunication is a bit different from circumcision, you nasty fuck," John said heatedly.

"Just saying," Toenails added, "them CO's ain't ever gonna let them come in here for that."

John looked at me, eyebrows arched. "His stupid is growing exponentially now." Then he looked back at

Toenails and said in a scathing voice, "I'm telling you, you need to cut them nasty claws, they are draining your powers. Pretty soon you're going to be a fucking slug staring at the lights and you're going to accidently cut yourself in half when you discover that you're attached to them claws."

John sat next to me on my boat. "How can they excommunicate you if you're already out?" he asked.

"Clearly when I called and asked to be removed from the church records they lied when they said they would," I said.

"Wait," Chomper added, "the church kicked you out? How come?"

"Because I'm in here," I said, as if it wasn't clearly obvious.

"Well that's illegal," he said making a whistling sound with his s-sounds. "A church can't kick you out just because you needs help. That's they's whole job, to be there for you when nobody else is. You could sue them for kicking you out when you need them most." He was completely serious.

"That's not how churches work where I come from." My words were flatter than the paper I held.

"So basically," John said in his narrative voice, "you broke up with them, and now they are coming around after all this time saying oh no no no motherfucker, we're breaking up with you."

"Pretty much," I replied.

"You should sue them man, yeah, you should sue them," Chomper said, agreeing with himself.

"Sorry Moon," John said as he stood up and left me alone with my letter. I folded it pensively and put it away in the gray cloud of my thoughts.

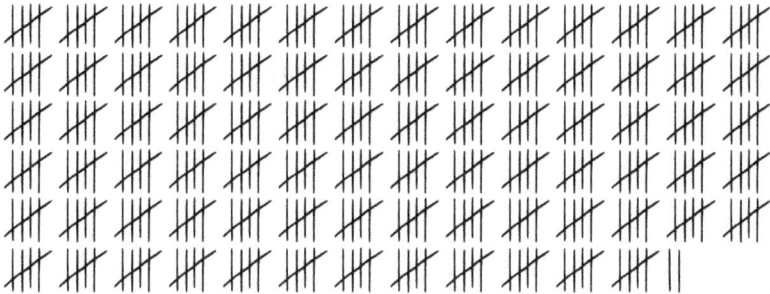

I recognized him the moment he walked into the pod. Due to my ever-worsening contacts, I couldn't really make out the face from my cell, but his shape and gait immediately reminded me of that time in the church service in Seminole County Jail. It was Martin's codefendant.

During pod time, I didn't have to wait long. He came immediately to me and leaned on the cement pillar next to where I was about to start my pushups.

"Sup?" he said. I tried to gauge if he recognized me at all. I got down and started my push-ups.

"I hear that you gave your girl the moon." He nodded his head trying to be cool. "Major props man," he added. "I'd love to be able to give my girl the moon." I ignored him and he brushed it off like he didn't notice.

I ran my lap up the stairs and around the circumference of the pod. When I returned to where I started he approached me again. "What the fuck is up with the food in here man? I mean I get that they are trying to save money and all, but what is this shit?"

Even though I knew he came from a place where the food was worse, I didn't want to give it away that I knew about him.

"You think peanut butter would be cheap enough to give us, at least put some protein in our diet," I said pretending to be invested in his conversation.

"I've never had any peanut butter," he said abruptly.

"What do you mean?" I asked.

"I mean," he said, drawing out his words, "I've never had peanut butter."

"Never, never" I asked, "or never in jail?"

"Never, never," he said, almost as if he was proud of it.

"How is that possible?" I asked. He didn't seem to understand my confusion.

"Just never had it," he said. "Didn't know it was a thing really."

I nodded in an attempt to mask the look of incredulity overcoming my face. I started doing my sit-ups, thinking about how Martin had really undersold his explanation that his codefendant had lived a privileged life.

"So uh..." he said, leaning down to get closer to me so his words didn't carry to too many listening ears. I hear you've got some moon rocks buried somewhere." He paused to see if this would get a reaction out of me. I just continued with my workout. "Super smart man, I would have done the same." I just continued doing sit-ups. When I finished he lowered his voice and said, "I was wondering if you might need some money."

He just stayed there waiting for me to respond. I

did my next round of push-ups and left for my next lap without addressing him. When I returned he was still there.

This time he waited for me to start my sit-ups, then he leaned in and whispered, "I could have forty K put on your books if you can deliver me enough moon dust to put in one of them snow globes, you know, so I can make something special for my girl."

I finished my set and then said, "Sure," calling his bluff. "You put forty thousand on my books, send me an address and I'll make sure it gets there."

His face lit up, like he was getting away with something. "Cool," he said. "I'll talk to my people and have it to you within a week."

He left, strangely satisfied, as if he was convinced that we were having a real conversation. An hour later he was called out for a lawyer visit. As soon as he was gone two officers came into the pod and took his stuff.

"Not a good sign," John said as he approached me.
"What?" I asked.

"That dude wasn't going to see his lawyer. Lawyer visits don't mean dressing out." He looked in my eyes and added, "What were you two talking about?" I didn't respond.

"Ah shit," he said, "you didn't... you know that rat was prolly wearing a wire. You didn't say anything important did you?"

"Roberts!" the officer yelled. "Laywer visit."

John looked at me, rolled his eyes and said, "Ah fuck."

...

My lawyer wasn't there. An attractive lady wearing a black dress suit and high heels, sat across the table from me next to a man in a pen-striped suit. I put my handcuffs under the table.

"Mister Roberts," she said as if it were the first day of school and she was setting the stage for a classroom wherein the only questions allowed were hers. "I'm the lead prosecutor of your case and I'm here to ask you some questions."

"Where is my lawyer?" I asked.

"He's not here," she said, offering no other information. I looked at her partner. He was just staring at me like I had just stabbed a love one of his and now it was time for his revenge.

"We are here to offer you the chance to help yourself," she said locking her eyes with mine. "You can help us help you, and tell us everything you know, in which case this will all go easier on you, or you can choose to not cooperate and I can promise you we will push for the maximum punishment."

I felt far less sickened this time, less intimidated. Instead I was flushed with disgust for having to be in her presence. I took a deep breath and looked past her.

"First off," she said, "we need you to tell us what you did with doctor Glibson's research notes."

Still looking past her, I replied in monotone with audible contempt. "Like I said before, everything that we took that we weren't arrested with, everything in the safe, was in a box in the storage unit, which the Feds have."

"What about the Mars rock, ALH eight four zero zero one?" she asked as she read the number off a piece of paper. "You stole that from doctor Glibson's office."

"It was with us when we got arrested," I said. I no longer cared if she was capable of following the logic.

"But the notebooks weren't there," she said. "What did you do with the notebooks?"

"Like I said before," I repeated, "everything in that safe was either with us when we got arrested or in the storage unit box. If the notebooks were taken by us, then they are now in the custody of the Feds."

"The Feds don't have the notebooks," she insisted. "Tell us what you did with them."

Looking forcefully into her eyes I said, "If they weren't there, then they weren't in the safe to begin with."

"Well then," she said rolling her eyes as she prepared for her sarcasm voice, "If the notebooks weren't in the safe, then why would doctor Glibson, a renowned NASA scientist, and upstanding citizen say that they were?"

"I don't know," I said. "Maybe he had more than just Martian meteorites tucked away where they weren't supposed to be. Maybe he had other moon rocks at home or somewhere and he wanted to bury the paper trail under my case. Or maybe he just has prosecutor blood in him and likes to hear animals squeal in pain as he kicks them, even after he has shot them down. Or maybe he just lost his notebooks at home somewhere, but mistakenly thought he put them in that safe."

Her partner leaned towards me with a violent jerk and in voice of distain said, "You expect us to believe you over him, after what you've done?"

"I don't care what you believe," I said, completely fed up. I stood up. "This meeting is over."

"Sit down Mister Roberts," the prosecutor said. I remained standing. She looked at me with pleasure in her eyes and said, "So tell us about the snow globe."

I rolled my eyes and sighed.

"That's right," she said. "We know all about it— about your continued criminal plans, and about the book you are writing to glorify your criminal actions." She looked at her partner. They both smiled. Then she added, "Tell us where you hid the moon rocks."

...

"What's going on?" John asked. I reached under my boat and grabbed the notepad. "What happened?" he added.

"They want to make a copy of my book draft," I said.

"That's fucking weird," he said. "That's it? Nothing else?" he asked.

"Well they thought that I was still in the moon rock market for a while, but they finally dropped that shit. Now they are hoping that something in here can make me look like the Hitler character they really want me to be."

"You know they're going to try to find ways to use every word in that against you, right?" he asked.

"The prosecutor is saying I have to," I said.

"What's you lawyer say?" he asked.

"Don't know," I said. "If you see him, ask him for me."

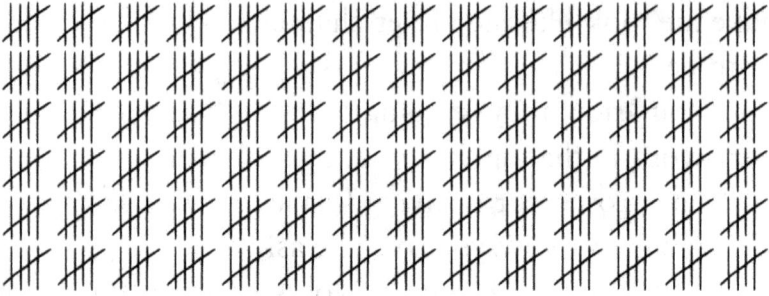

"Shit this? I don't care about this. Look at me, I'm an old timer. I done had my day, fucked all the girls I'm gonna fuck, done all the shit I'm gonna do." He played his card then continued. "I wasn't getting out of the house much anyway with this fucking hip. Just last month I was thinking a change of scenery might do me some good. Wasn't thinking this exactly, but shit who are we kidding? What was there to look forward to any way? Wasn't having any sex, probably going to a rest home soon, the most shit stained kind out there, cause I can't afford better. So in a way this... this is my rest home."

"Not me," a red haired man said. "Got my best years stolen from me, ripped away by that god damned rat. Now I'm gonna be wasting away in here, smelling farts and listening to snoring all night, while all the hot ass babes in the world be a thousand miles away, and I'm in here rubbing my dick down to nothing just trying to remember what girls look like.

"If you want to know what girls be like," the hillbilly said, "open your mouth and close your eyes. I'll make it something you won't forget for the rest of your bit."

"I said look like, you sick fuck," Ginger responded. "Besides," he said with a smirk," I heard from your bunky that you ain't got nothin' there any ways. Says your pubes is longer than your pole." The Old Timer began to laugh, but the laugh quickly turned into a cough.

...

Nobody was sleeping. There was a shared sense of anxiety filling the whole pod. Another hour passed and the officer decided to make the rounds again.

"Seriously? Where the fuck we gonna go?" one of the inmates yelled as the officer passed his cell. "You really need to check that we are here still?" he added. The officer ignored him. "Think one of us escaped during the last hour, just walked through the walls and shit?" The officer continued his count. "Fuck, you know what?" he taunted through the bars. "This place ain't nothing like the brochure. I want a refund."

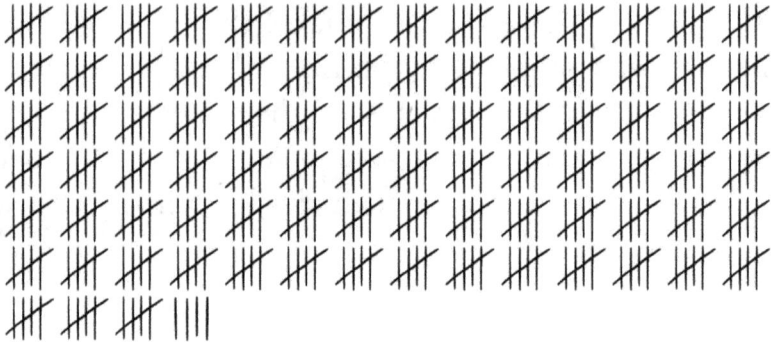

"Roberts!" the CO yelled. I approached his desk trying to determine from his face if I was in trouble for something.

"I've been instructed to tell you to call your wife," he said, half distracted by the magazine he was reading.

My heart began racing. Did something happen to her? Did she change her mind and decide to sign me out? Did she decide she wants to be together after all? Why was she requesting communication now? After all of these months of not accepting my calls... why now? And how did she get this message passed to me? I had never heard of someone delivering a message through a CO like this. What was going on?

I went to the phones on the pillars and nervously dialed the number.

"This call is from a federal inmate," the electronic voice announced. "To block this call press seven now. To accept the charges press five..."

She accepted the charges.

"Hello?" I said.

I could barely hear her voice over the background noise of yelling in my pod. I pressed the phone into my

250

ear as tightly as I could and plugged my other ear with my finger.

"Are you having fun with your new friends?" she asked in a very happy, yet naïve way.

I didn't know what to say. I'd never known her to be sarcastic... was she serious?

"What?" I asked.

"Are you having fun with your new friends?" she repeated.

I paused, trying to understand the question.

"Never mind," she said, "It's none of my business."

"I was told you wanted me to call?" I said with a lump in my throat.

"Oh, yes," she said in a way that sounded like she was doing something with her hands and holding the phone between her shoulder and ear. "I just wanted to tell you that I have sent you the divorce papers, so you can be ready to sign them right away, you know, get some stamps or whatever you have to do. If I got them back by the weekend, that would be great. Otherwise it might end up ruining next week for me. Okay?"

I was flushed with confusion. Her fake happy go lucky attitude felt like the coldest thing in the world to me? I suddenly felt sick.

"Okay?" she repeated.

"Thanks for letting me know," I said, with tears running down my face. It felt like she was about to hang up. I took a deep breath and asked, "Are you happy?"

"Of course," she said casually. "Look, Thad, I'm in the middle of something so I have to go okay? Good luck with your life and thanks for signing the papers right away."

She hung up. I stayed in position, holding the phone to my ear, and keeping my other arm up plugging my ear and blocking my face as I cried.

卌 卌 卌 卌 卌 卌 卌 卌 卌 卌 卌 卌 卌 卌
卌 卌 卌 卌 卌 卌 卌 卌 卌 卌 卌 卌 卌 卌
卌 卌 卌 卌 卌 卌 卌 卌 卌 卌 卌 卌 卌 卌
卌 卌 卌 卌 卌 卌 卌 卌 卌 卌 卌 卌 卌 卌
卌 卌 卌 卌 卌 卌 卌 卌 卌 卌 卌 卌 卌 卌
卌 卌 卌 卌 卌 卌 卌 卌 卌 卌 卌 卌 卌 卌
卌 卌 卌 卌 卌 卌

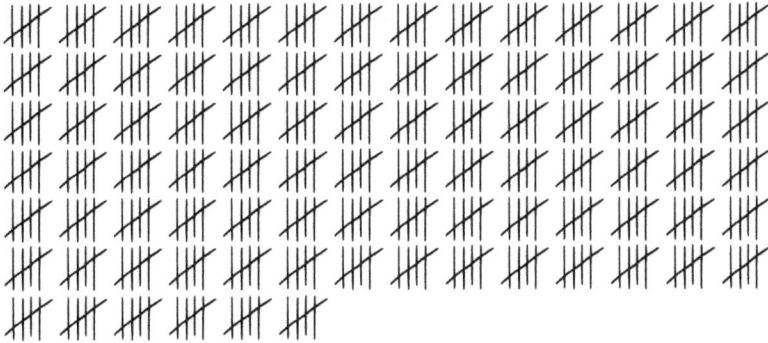

After lights out, the officer on duty set himself up to watch a movie on his portable player.

"Hey, CO. CO!" one of the inmates across the pod yelled out.

"What do you need?" the officer replied.

"How's about you let us listen to some music?"

"I don't think you want to listen to my music," the officer replied.

"Shit man, I ain't heard music in over a year. I'll listen to anything," the prisoner said.

The officer was quiet for a bit and then said, "Okay, but I'm playing only one song and then I want no trouble tonight. Understand me?"

"You're the boss, boss," the inmate said.

The officer unplugged his headphones from his entertainment unit and fiddled with it. All the murmuring in the pod trailed off. I had never heard the place so quiet. The sound of strings and a mellow beat began to softly fill the pod. The officer turned the volume up and sat on his desk.

I closed my eyes, absorbing every note of a song I had never heard before. Had I forgotten that music felt like this? Did it always have this encompassing and transformative power? I couldn't remember.

The notes beautifully echoed throughout the chamber—connecting me to something I had lost, to a spark of life that gave rise to just enough defiance to actually claim a life. Self-proclaimed gangsters, hoodlums, niggas, convicts, hard men, revealed what was beneath that hard shell. For one song we were the same, scared and lost, carried by the sound of Dido's voice to a different life... "I will go down with this ship. And I won't put my hands up and surrender. There will be no white flag above my door. I'm in love and always will be..."

I closed my eyes and felt my entire body become flooded with nerve endings that conjured up vivid wisps of past memories. I remembered what it was like to have the freedom to make mistakes without being crippled of fear. Did she know how I still felt about her? Did she still remember? Was she okay?

I turned to my side, facing the bars, letting the tears run off my cheek. When the song was over the officer sat down in his chair, reconnected his headphones and put them on. The whole pod remained completely silent. I drifted to sleep behind my bars, frozen in desperation of shattered hope, slipping further and further into an empty future.

...

After sawing through the locking pins, we slowly opened the safe door. It was obvious that we were nervous and excited. We both held our breath as we pulled it the rest of the way off. We looked inside. A lid on one of the vials had come off, causing moon dust to spill. I looked at Tiffany, licked my finger and then rolled my finger in the pile of dust. Then, just as quickly, I put my finger in my mouth and cleaned it off.

She looked at me, her eyes dancing between both of mine. I pulled my finger back out and she kissed me.

Then she looked at me reassuringly and said, "This will always be with you." I touched her face with my right hand and we kissed passionately. Then she gracefully moved to place her lips next to my ear. Her golden hair felt so soft. She gently added, "Always."

I woke up. Light from the little hole in the window was hitting my face. I got out of my boat, climbed into the window, and stood on my tiptoes to see out.

The light was coming from the moon—still circling the heavens and watching over the world, undimmed and unharmed.

‖ ‖ ‖ ‖ ‖ ‖ ‖ ‖ ‖ ‖ ‖ ‖ ‖ ‖
‖ ‖ ‖ ‖ ‖ ‖ ‖ ‖ ‖ ‖ ‖ ‖ ‖ ‖
‖ ‖ ‖ ‖ ‖ ‖ ‖ ‖ ‖ ‖ ‖ ‖ ‖ ‖
‖ ‖ ‖ ‖ ‖ ‖ ‖ ‖ ‖ ‖ ‖ ‖ ‖ ‖
‖ ‖ ‖ ‖ ‖ ‖ ‖ ‖ ‖ ‖ ‖ ‖ ‖ ‖
‖ ‖ ‖ ‖ ‖ ‖ ‖ ‖ ‖ ‖ ‖ ‖ ‖ ‖
‖ ‖ ‖ ‖ ‖ ‖ ‖ |||

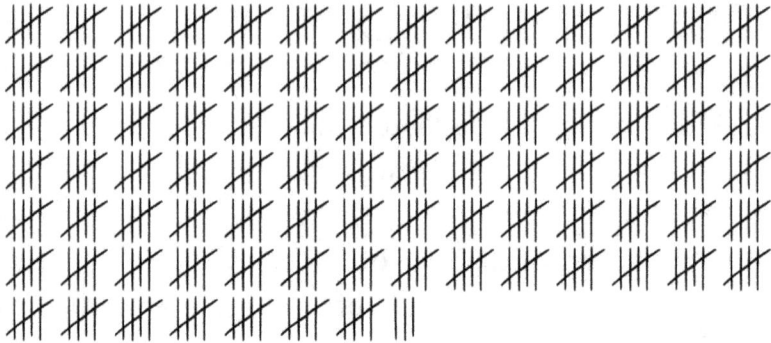

"What's up, Moon? You okay?" John asked.

I pulled the cell door closed behind me, sat down on my boat, and took off my blue BoBos—the one dollar clown shoes I had been issued for court. "The fucking razor man," I said frustrated and angry.

"What razor?" John asked.

I reached under my mattress and pulled it out. "I saved this razor for weeks," I said. "Made it through at least ten shake downs with this damn thing, and then they go and call me at four in the morning, with no warning, and give me no chance of cleaning up first. I was going to be all clean and shaved..." I started choking up and turned away so he wouldn't see. Everyone in the room stayed quiet.

"I sat in that damn holding cell for four hours before we even left. There was no reason to be in such a hurry," I added.

"Did they sentence you?" John asked.

"No," I replied softly.

"Then you still got another chance," he said.

"It's not that," I said. I tried to breathe deeply to regain my composure.

John walked closer, but stopped at the edge of his bunk.

After a long pause I continued, "She didn't even look at me man." Tears were welling up in my eyes.

John just looked at me without saying a word.

I grabbed my orange outfit in my fists and said, "I was wearing this piece of shit costume, handcuffed, looking like a criminal. She was behind me and they were all talking so fast, dressed in suits and dresses. I couldn't even hear what they were saying. All I could think about was her. I couldn't take it any longer so I turned around to look at her, but she looked down. She just kept looking down."

"It's just a fuck'n hoe dawg," Cue Ball said lying down on his bed.

John looked at him and said, "You're like a motherfucking goldfish, you know that. Going 'round and 'round your bowl, saying the same damn things every time you open your motherfucking mouth."

"Just saying," Cue Ball said.

John looked back at me and I continued.

"My lawyer was tugging on my arm. She had dyed her hair purple, had a new nose ring, she looked defiant and sexy, and she was right there... right there." I wiped the tears falling down my face.

"She probably just didn't want the judge to know that she still cares about you, Moon Rock. You said she's a smart girl. She's just playing it smart," John said.

"I know, I know," I said. "But her face..." I said. "I think..."

"Don't start thinking like that, Moon Rock," John said. "You got to let go of all that dreaming, hoping, and wishing. The future's gonna come no matter what, but you're going to miss it when it gets here if you don't learn how to see the present."

I looked up at him as he sat down on my boat and asked, "So, what did you get for lunch?"

I wiped my cheeks with the back of my hands. After a long pause I said, "You really know how to focus on the positive."

"Shit man," John said. "You're down long enough you realize that in here, when everything you care about is taken away, all that's left is the positive."

Chomper chimed in with his whistling tooth. "That's right. When you're lower than a snake's belly, all there is, is up." Laying on his bunk he rolled onto his stomach and arched his back, pretending to be a snake looking at the sky.

John leaned in closer, demanding more direct attention. "You're still trying to hold on to them things that they already took. You're doing exactly what they want you to do, living in the past, stressing out about the future. Shit, as soon as you wake up, as soon as you realize that all that shit was never yours to begin with..." He put his hands next to his face and spread his fingers. "You're free."

I looked at him like he was crazy. "Time is a gift man," he said. "That judge don't have no time, them prosecutors don't have no time. And you, you spent most of your time chasing your own damn tail just like the rest of them."

He twisted his body to more fully face me. "Look, one day you'll be in prison…"

"Great," I interrupted, "I have such a bright future to look forward to."

John hit me hard on the shoulder and said, "Man this shit is for real. You don't want to listen, that's on you, but I'm gonna give it to straight you just in case you ever decide you fuckin' tired of being locked up in your mind."

I scolded him with my eyes as I rubbed the sharp sting in my shoulder.

"Okay," he continued, repositioning himself. "If you don't learn what free really is, then some day you're gonna be in prison, under the sun looking up and watching planes going by. And when that day comes you're gonna think to yourself, if only I was on that plane instead of being here, trapped in this place, then I'd be happy. And then one day you'll be out, and you'll end up on one of those planes, flying over people below that are looking up wishing they was somewhere else, in a different life, an important life, going somewhere important. But instead of celebrating that you've made it, and being blissfully happy with your life, you know what you'll be doing when that moment comes? You'll be worried about the meeting you're going to. Will it go well? Am I prepared? Did I impress the right people… The fucking game is the same no matter what level you're on. It's rigged to keep you unhappy, to keep you always looking up and reaching for something else, thinking your shit is just around the corner, just one more promotion, a bigger raise, more power, more money, more respect... It's all fucked. Those people in those planes are just as trapped as you are right now. There's only one way to be free in this world. Only one."

The room was quiet for several seconds.

"Well?" I asked.

"Well what?" he replied.

"Are you going to tell me what that one way is?"

He laughed and said, "that ain't for me to say, Moon Rock, you've got to figure it out for yourself. But I can give you a hint." He leaned in closer and whispered. "Free people see past all of this." He made a circle with his finger. "They ain't squinting their eyes trying to get back into the past. They ain't hurrying themselves up on some sprint to the future. They just take the one thing that really exists and then let it go.

Chomper started laughing. "Hey guys, look at me, I'm a snake on a plane."

"You're one tooth away from a perfect blow job, that's what you are," John declared with conviction as if he was waiting for Chomper to memorize this new title. Then he switched to a cheerful tone and asked, "So, what did you get in the courthouse?" as he went for another shoulder punch.

I blocked his punch, making him smile.

260

"A bologna sandwich and a little bag of Lays chips," I said.

He jumped up excited. "Ah shit man. Mmmmmmm mmmmm. Imagine that. Meat-like substance that has a motherfucking name. Real chips." He looked at our other bunkies, cocked his head towards me, and then, in a voice that parodied conspiracy, but was intentionally loud enough for all to hear, he said, "Sometimes I think about killing one of these motherfuckers just to start another case so I can go to court and get me a real sandwich."

Cue Ball and Chomper ignored him, but Toenails looked at him and raised his eyebrows.

John started laughing. "Don't worry, Toenails," he said. "I'd have killed your nasty ass a long time ago, but I realized them claws will just keep on growing."

. . .

"Roberts!" the pod officer yelled as he was walking up the stairs to my cell. I looked at John and shrugged my shoulders. I stood up and waited for him. He approached my door and lowered his voice, "Thought you'd be interested to know that your girl got probation."

"Seriously?" I asked.

"It's on the news," he replied.

"Thank you. Thank you very much," I said.

He nodded and went back downstairs to his desk.

261

I turned around and saw John standing there with his hand up waiting for a high five. I went for it and then started laughing and pacing around the room.

"What did I tell you?" John said as he climbed back in his bed. "No news is good news." He pointed his finger at me and said, "But good news is even better."

I stepped up into the window, trying to see out the little hole.

"See anything interesting?" John asked.

"The alligator is gone," I said.

"Ahhh shit." John replied. "You hear that Toenails? Moon Rock's girl is free, your snarl-jawed cousin done moved on to a better place. Things are looking up."

"Muthafucka," Toenails replied. "Why the cock-a-dial gots to be my cousin?"

"Is that a joke?" John asked, pointing both hands at Toenails and widening his eyes.

"Fuck you, muthafuck'n white trash hillbilly."

"I'm just fucking with you man," John said as he folded his arms and laid down. "Your skin ain't thick enough to be cousins with no crocodile, and your feet are way too snarled up and nasty to survive in the wild."

Toenails turned his back to John and didn't reply.

"You keep staring out dat hole like you'd trying to figure out what's out der," Cue Ball said. "Shit I'll tell you what's out der. Chicken! Motha fucking chicken, dat's what. Chicken wings, watermelon, and collared greens! And ain't none of it gonna get any closer by you staring out that hole." I slowly returned to my familiar spot, took a deep breath, and fell deeply asleep in my boat.

𝍷𝍷𝍷𝍷 𝍷𝍷𝍷𝍷 𝍷𝍷𝍷𝍷 𝍷𝍷𝍷𝍷 𝍷𝍷𝍷𝍷 𝍷𝍷𝍷𝍷 𝍷𝍷𝍷𝍷 𝍷𝍷𝍷𝍷 𝍷𝍷𝍷𝍷 𝍷𝍷𝍷𝍷 𝍷𝍷𝍷𝍷 𝍷𝍷𝍷𝍷 𝍷𝍷𝍷𝍷 𝍷𝍷𝍷𝍷

(tally marks — seven rows counting the days)

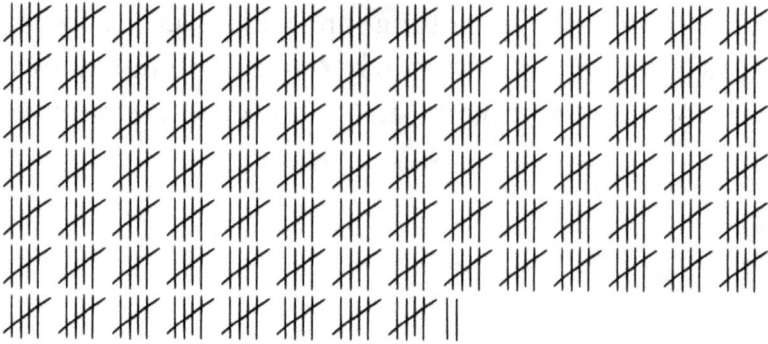

"Good luck," John said as I left the cell. The rest of my cellmates gave me a nod.

"Remember," Toenails said, "twenty-foe," as he shook his hand. "I'm counting on it."

"I hope you're right," I said.

I walked down the stairs slowly, revisiting all the probability charts I had worked up in my head.

"You ready?" the CO asked.

"I was ready fifteen months ago," I said with confidence.

"How many times is this?" he asked.

"The ninth," I said.

"Well," he said with a bit of compassion, "Hopefully the ninth one is the charm."

He put handcuffs on me but didn't put on the leg shackles. I followed him to the R&D section of the jail, the waiting area for all incoming and outgoing prisoners. I was beginning to recognize the layout. As we approached the holding cells the officer instructed me to stand still. As he was opening my cell I looked across the hall.

Through a small window I saw a large man in a straightjacket, strapped into a chair mounted permanently in the middle of the room. His face was covered with a barred *Silence of the Lambs* mask that would normally make it difficult to tell exactly who it was, but with one look I knew. His dreadlocks and size gave it away. Dread didn't look up at me.

"Get in," the officer said, holding open my cell door. He locked me in and then walked across the hall and swung the metal cover over Dread's window shut.

My hands were still cuffed in front of me. I looked around and noticed an unopened condom floating in the toilet. I sat down on the cement bench and started waiting.

...

Returning down the 'tunnel of despair' towards my pod later that afternoon felt different this time. The bright lights, concrete walls and a polished floor of that long hallway felt extra reflective and uncluttered.

"Move it," the officer said without even looking at me. He had cuffed my ankles and now wanted me to walk faster than the cuffs would allow. He didn't seem all that bright, and he certainly didn't notice the faint smile on my face as I continued my steady pace.

The officer stood with his back to me as we waited in silence for the sally port door to close behind us. 'At what point did this actually become home?' I wondered as I stood in the hallway outside the pod.

The pod was locked down. Dozens of men were standing up in their cages, looking at me. I felt it in my chest first, then it got louder and louder. The beat was rhythmic like a distant chant, or faded war cry.

The door opened and the words became clear. "Moon Rock! Moon Rock! Moon Rock!" The officer removed my chains and I stepped inside. I walked to the middle of the room completely relaxed for the first time in fifteen months.

"Well what happened?" one of them yelled.

I stood there, no longer in a hurry, took a deep breath, absorbing the fact that the waiting and stressing about the unknown was finally over.

"Spit it out, Moon Rock," an inmate yelled.

"One hundred months," I said casually.

"Ah hell no. Ain't no fucking way!" one voice proclaimed.

"Seriously, what happened?" another asked.

I slowly looked around the pod and repeated, "One hundred months."

"Then why are you smiling?" someone yelled.

"Yeah, what the fuck, tell us for real."

I looked at the pod officer. He seemed just as curious as the rest and made no attempt to rush me to my cell. I walked to the stairs anyway and went to my cell. When I reached the top of the stairs the officer buzzed my door open.

"Come on man. Stop fucking with us. Tell us for real," said a prisoner from across the pod.

I closed the cell door behind me. All of my bunkies were eyeballing me like I was about to reveal a magic key that would make women want to have sex with you.

"You seem happy," John said.

"It's over," I replied.

"So what happened?" he asked.

I shrugged my shoulders and said, "One hundred months."

John started laughing. "For real?"

I gave him an affirmative look.

"Shit man," John said, "even I didn't expect that." Then he looked at our other bunkies, still laughing and said, "Ya'll motherfuckers are going to be sore tomorrow."

They all looked at me, still wondering if I was lying.

I looked at the back of my hand, at the number I had written on it.

"What's that?" John asked.

"It's her number," I said.

"Her, her? As in Tiffany?" he asked.

"Yup," I said.

"Good for you," said with a smile. "Well boys," he said to the rest of the room, "might as well get this shit over with."

John got down on the floor and started doing push-ups.

"Fuck!" Toenails said. He got down and started doing push-ups too. I got down on the floor too and started doing mine. The other two reluctantly followed.

At five 'o clock the news came on. A crowd patiently watched below for the report.

"Hey, hey, hey, here it is," one proclaimed. Everyone quieted down.

The report was quite clear, 'Judge triples sentence in Moon Rock case.'

"Holy shit!" someone exclaimed. The whole pod went up in a roar and then everyone got down to start doing push-ups.

"Hey, Moon Rock, how much for twenty-four?" a prisoner from the floor below yelled at me.

"Twenty-four is off by seventy-six," I said. "So you've got to do seven hundred and sixty."

"That's some fucked up shit man!" he replied.

At ten o' clock we were back in our cells. John, Cue Ball and I had finished earlier. Chomper got down to finish the rest of his and then was barely able to climb up to his top bunk. When he got there he crashed and began holding his arms.

Toenails was only at five hundred and fifty-three and he had cheated his way through most of those.

"I can't..." he said breathing hard and shaking.

We cheered him on, "Toenails! Toenails! Toenails!" He got down and wobbled his way up for one more push-up.

"Five fifty-four," we said. "I can't," he said falling to the floor.

"It's those damn nasty claws," John said. "I told you they're draining your power. You need to cut those motherfuckers off."

Toenails turned his head a little, like he wanted to say something, but then gave up. He collapsed on the ground, belly down with his feet in the air.

"Here," John added as he moved towards Toenails. "Let me yank those muthafuckas out for ya."

Toenails swatted at John with his claws. John jumped back and recoiled his face in disgust.

"Did you see that?" John said looking at me. "He just tried to give me his herpa-gono-syphli-aids from those nasty ass disease slicers."

For the next three hours we watched Toenails cheat his way through the rest of his push-ups.

Lying in bed after it was all over John said, "Hey, Toenails?"

There was no reply.

John raised his foot high and then slammed it down on his bed to make more noise and said, "Toenails!"

"What?" Toenails said softly.

"Since you ain't going to be able to pick up your tray tomorrow, can I have your meals?"

"Fuck you," Toenails replied still in pain.

Exhausted, we all lay in silence. After a few minutes John said, "Hey, Moon Rock."

I was looking into the pod through the bars. "Yeah?" I replied without turning my head.

"It's gonna to be okay man. They can't take nothing else from you no more. It's gonna be okay."

CHAPTER 5: CON AIR

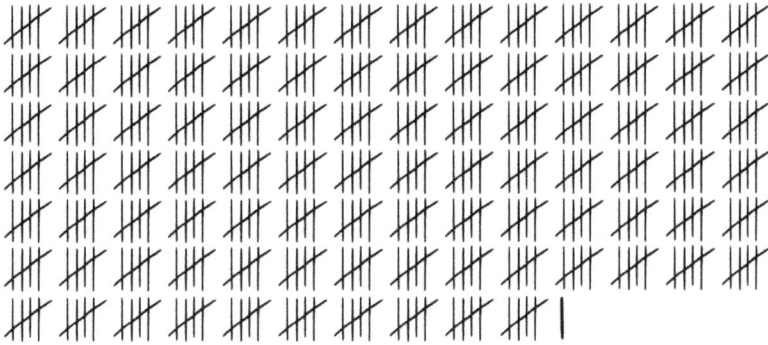

卌 卌 卌 卌 卌 卌 卌 卌 卌 卌 卌 卌 卌 卌
卌 卌 卌 卌 卌 卌 卌 卌 卌 卌 卌 卌 卌 卌
卌 卌 卌 卌 卌 卌 卌 卌 卌 卌 卌 卌 卌 卌
卌 卌 卌 卌 卌 卌 卌 卌 卌 卌 卌 卌 卌 卌
卌 卌 卌 卌 卌 卌 卌 卌 卌 卌 卌 卌 卌 卌
卌 卌 卌 卌 卌 卌 卌 卌 卌 卌 卌 卌 卌 卌
卌 卌 卌 卌 卌 卌 卌 卌 卌 卌 |

John shook me awake. "What?" I asked.

He was standing at the side of my boat with a calm face. "I'm getting transferred," he said. "They just called me."

I got out of my boat and stood up. He grabbed both of my shoulders, looked me straight in the eyes and said, "Remember, knock 'em dead. Love, have all your adventures, but don't forget what's most important."

I nodded at him. He waited, searching my eyes, then nodded back.

The door buzzed open. John rolled up his bedroll, nodded at me, and then exited as if it were just a regular day. He didn't look back.

The pod felt empty, as if a background essence I had never noticed before had lost its scent. The pit of my stomach was twisting, as if the rest of the universe was drifting away and there was nothing I could do to stop it. In my past life, the feeling of drifting off into space had been an academic curiosity—a fantasy to chase. But this was a far cry from pretending to drift off into the heavens as I launched off the edge of the International Space Station mock-up. The despair was visceral and paralyzing.

Hours passed with nothing happening, except for the occasional person climbing out of their bunk to go piss. Then the new recruits arrived. Two mangled souls stepped inside their new jungle, the portal to the rest of existence behind them. I stared at them, trying to guess which one would be replacing John.

One was Mexican, short and stocky, with a swagger that was meant to portray confidence. It was clear he was terrified. The other was a white man probably in his late twenties. I squinted my eyes, trying to get a better look. There was something off about him, almost as if he wasn't scared, worried, or even put out by being here. "Impossible," I thought. "It must be my filmy contacts."

Our door popped open, along with a door downstairs.

"Gonzales," the CO yelled, pointing to the room downstairs. I got a cold shiver as the CO pointed to our room while looking at the other man. He started walking up the stairs.

Toenails was pretending to sleep, but the rest of us were sitting up. The new guy latched the door behind himself and walked to the open bed. "Okay boys," he said. "Guess it's your motherfucking lucky day." He wasn't looking at any one in particular. He unrolled his bedroll but didn't seem interested in tying the sheets the right way.

"Oh," Cue Ball said as he laid down putting his hands behind his head, "I can feel my luck changing already."

Picking up on the sarcasm, the new guy leaned down to his new bunky and said, "That wasn't a threat my man. You just gonna want to have me on your side, that's all." He looked around the room and added, "You're all gonna want my advice, trust me. See, I know how to work the system, done beat it already. I can save you all a lot of trouble."

"You's a bad ass muthafucka huh?" Toenails said with a laugh, keeping his eyes closed.

The new guy's face went cold. With a slightly tilted head, he glared at Toenails, as if he was shooting lightning bolts at him with his imagination. "That's right," he said.

"Look more like some chomo to me, like a Hannibal Lector fuck," Chomper said.

The new guy leaned into Chomper, putting his face just inches away from Chomper's single tooth and said, "Then I suggest you pick your words more carefully."

He lingered there for a couple of seconds, then suddenly stood up straight and lightly said, "You see, I was originally arrested for murder." He was animating his words with his hands and a proud face. "They thought I was part of this gang, that I worked for this big guy, that had killed someone. And they thought I might have been involved with him. Put me on his case and all." He turned towards the fogged over window and faced it as if he were actually looking outside.

"They came at me with that usual shit, you know the game," he raised the pitch of his voice to mimic the prosecutors. "Cooperate and we will go easy on you, don't cooperate and we will fuck you hard."

"Shit," he continued. "Did they think I was falling for that?" He laughed to himself then turned around with excitement in his eyes. "Get this... My lawyer comes to me, right? Starts talking 'bout some Proffer agreement. You ever heard of that shit? Well I'm telling you it's completely legit. Basically the prosecutors put in writing that if you help them out, giving them information and answering all their questions, then whatever you tell them they can't charge you with, no way, no how. If you spit it out right then, well then they can't touch you."

He spun around and looked at Chomper. "I know what you're thinking," he said. "It's a trap, just another one of their games, but motherfucker, I'm telling you this thing is air tight." He sat down on the foot of Toenail's bunk. Toenails had opened his eyes now. It was obvious that Toenails was uncomfortable with this, but he didn't say anything.

"I'm telling you God really had my back," he added raising both hands up. "You think you're on one path in life, done fucked up and shit, and then God lets you know that He still has plans for you. It was obvious that He was giving me a chance to be completely free as long as I told them everything. So," he said as he looked back and forth at the faces in the room, "my lawyer looks it over, makes sure that bitch is as tight as a whore's grip on a twenty dollar bill and then I sit down and tell them. I tell them everything, man." He laughs loudly this time.

"They signed that agreement 'cause they thought this other guy was killing all them people, put it right in my lap. You see that's how you got to play them." He was still laughing.

"I looked them right in the eyes and told 'em it was me. I killed those people, every single one of them. I answered all their questions, told them how I killed them, told them why, gave them the whole truth, like a confession you know? It was cleansing. And now I'm wiped clean, brand new, like a baptized baby."

He was bobbing his head back and forth as he talked. "See, they thought they was after some other guy, right? I'm telling you, God works in mysterious ways. Ain't nothing like that happen for no reason. God has big plans for me." He directed his next command at Cue Ball, with confident eyes. "That's why you want me on your side."

He stood back up and started pacing in the cell, continuing his story. "They didn't know shit, really, but I took that opportunity to give it all to them. I told 'em I was an enforcer. It was my job to make sure all the people out there stayed honest and didn't cheat nobody, trying to skip out on their payments and shit." He recalled his past with a face beaming of self-satisfaction.

"Shit I was good at my job," he added. "Never personal, just professional." He walked over to the toilet, pulled out his cock and started pissing while continuing his story.

"Hell, this one time some dude was two weeks behind on paying for his shit, he done smoked it all, and he was given a warning after one week. They came to me and told me his name, gave me his address, told me to take care of it. Did I flinch? No," he said as if he were confused about whether he was aiming for Drill Sergeant or Preacher, "not for a second. That shit was in God's hands now."

He flushed and walked back between the bunk beds. There was an aloof disconnect in how he acted out his story with his body language, as if his emotional bank had been scrambled and randomized. "So I went to the place, found an open window in the back and waited. Two, maybe three hours, I ate some food out the fridge, sat there patiently in the kitchen, just letting God's holy spirit pass through me, guide me, being open to whatever, you know?"

He had his back to the window now, hunched over a little with his hands in front of him. "Then I heard him coming in the front door with a little girl and God whispered his plan to me. So I tied them both up and took one of the knives the lord had provided from the kitchen, and I cut off one of the little bitch's fingers off." He acted out the stabbing and turning of the knife.

"Then I was about to cut off one of his fingers just to make sure it done sunk in, but God let me know I had done his will."

He looked around quickly, "He warned me, you know? Told me to look outside the window, so I did and saw cop lights down the street. I took off like a bat out of hell, bolting out the back, jumped the fence in one hop and disappeared clean. God really had my back man, I'm telling you. And you know what? Motherfucker paid that shit the next day."

"God had your back?" I said.

My cellmates were looking at me and shaking their heads.

"What?" I said raising my voice. "We're supposed to just sit here and take that shit from this sick fuck just because he's fucking crazy?"

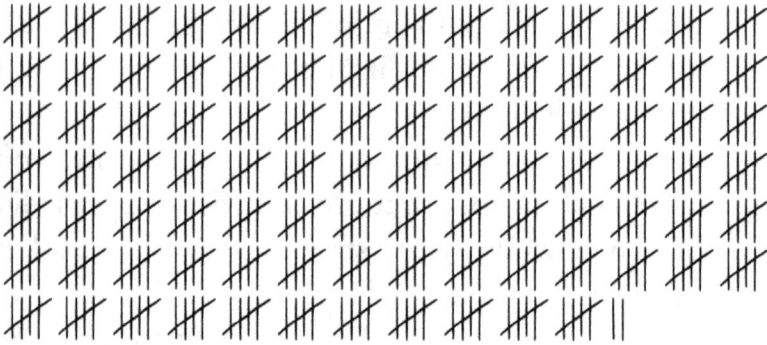

"Roberts!" the CO yelled. "Pack your shit." I took a deep breath. I hadn't gotten any real sleep in weeks now. It had been a constant stream of threats and veiled threats from Hannibal. At first, Cue Ball thought his story was just bullshit, but then we learned from the newspaper that his story was true, and that the prosecutor's hands were tied and they ended up charging him for something he left out, a simple theft, for which the maximum sentence was five years, so he was given five years. But there was no deep sleeping around him. My cellmates and I tried to set up shifts, but we never really relaxed enough to get any real sleep.

The door popped open. I was already holding my bedroll waiting. I looked back inside and gave Cue Ball, Chomper and Toenails a head nod while avoiding Hannibal's cold eyes. Cue Ball nodded back. Chomper gave me a peace sign, and Toenails wiggled his nasty springs at me one last time.

278

...

The outside world seemed so busy. The officer parked the van and got out. There were at least eight cars with flashing lights and at least two not-so-hidden snipers on top of nearby buildings. The side door opened and I waited my turn to scoot out of the van. The only way to get out was to hop out with both feet at the same time.

It felt surreal standing there on the tarmac in bright orange prison coveralls and blue BoBo's, shackled at the ankles and wrists, and belly chained. The cool air and warm sunlight triggered flash memories of Utah through my mind, hiking up canyons, following the cliface.

"Ahhhh," the prisoner next to me exclaimed as he stretched his neck, closed his eyes and felt the Sun on his face. "How long has it been?" he asked.

"Since I was locked up?" I asked.

"No, since you've had the Sun on your face," he said.

I was quiet for a moment and said "Sixteen months." The prisoner on the other side of him joined the conversation and said, "Nineteen for me."

"You two are lucky," he said with his eyes still closed. "I fought my case. It's been thirty-eight months for me."

I joined him and closed my eyes and tilted my face towards the Sun. There were several traces in the air, including a faint smell of cut grass. I recalled a much younger me using a Mason jar to catch bees that were fascinated with the dandelions in my front yard.

The Sun was brighter than I remembered, making my eyes water even when they were closed. The wind was a bit cold and unfamiliar. It felt like a dream, being surrounded by things blowing in the wind, having the horizon be so far off into the distance, standing under the sky.

"Move!" one of the officers commanded. We began clinking along, shuffling our feet in tune, trying to make this brief exposure to the outdoors last longer. The shiny glint of the airplane sparked memories of my first flight—how excited and nervous I was as I turned from base to final that first time. I was concentrating so hard as the runway came closer and closer, flexing my arms as tight as I could to hold the yoke, with no understanding of the trim tab. Had it been real? Were my memories tricking me? It all seemed so long ago. The excitement slipped away like spilled moon dust.

Shoulder to shoulder we stood in the shadow of the airplane as the officers herded a few dozen prisoners off it. Several officers were tightly gripping their shotguns with both hands, with the faces of glim statues.

"Do you think a scowl is a required part of the uniform?" I asked the guy who fought his case.

"That and a stick up the ass," he said quietly enough to not be heard by the nearest officer. Several officers paced back and forth, watching us like they were desperate for just one of us to do something that would warrant them taking us all out.

The prisoner who had fought his case looked at me and said, "I didn't know I was this dangerous." Several of us started to laugh.

The guards were unamused. We tried to stop laughing, but it was hard to hold it in. It was also growing harder and harder to ignore the increasingly urgent feeling from my bladder.

We lined up in the shadow of the airplane and watched the inmates awkwardly descend the stairs, contorting their bodies with exaggerated motions in an attempt to save the bony protrusions of their legs from being cut by the metal cuffs.

A slender black man, with cornrow hair, was near the front of our line dancing back and forth from one foot to the other, presumably in an attempt to stay warm.

After the last prisoner cleared the stairs, an officer at the bottom gave the first prisoner in our line the head nod, signaling for him to start the climb to the airplane's entrance. The slender black man began to freak out.

"I'm not getting on that." He said, refusing to move forward.

One of the officers saw the growing gap in our line. "Move it," he commanded as he walked closer.

"Hell no, un uh, I ain't doing it. I ain't supposed to be on no plane. It ain't natural," the slender man said.

Holding up the line turned out to be a very effective way to agitate this funeral squad. Several officers approached him from different directions.

"You either get on that plane, or we will put you on it," the biggest one said, daring him to challenge his order. The prisoner didn't move.

The big brute smiled and nodded with excitement, thrilled by the process of submission that he now felt authorized to engage in. Two other officers joined him, grabbing their newest victim and forcing him up the stairs. He fought back, screaming and throwing his body every way he could. One officer tried picking him up by his ankle chains, metal cutting into his legs, while two others grabbed his upper body. He was screaming and wiggling about. Then he began kicking, despite the shackles.

He kicked so hard that the lead officer didn't feel confident dragging him up the stairs. They lowered him back down and forced him to the ground. He was still screaming incoherently and thrashing about in terror. They proudly held him down.

A female officer approached with a metal box in her hands. She opened it and took out a needle. She held the needle in front of his face, pausing for several seconds, showing him the needle and smiling. Then she stuck it in his shoulder. They continued to hold him down until he had no fight left.

One of the officers got up and approached our line. "Anyone else got a problem with getting on the plane?" he yelled.

We all knew to not look at him. One foot at a time we made our way up the metal stairs. With every step the shackles twisted and cut into me. I tried to find a better way to make the ascent, but the shackles were chained too close together.

At the top I was surprised to find that Con Air looked a lot like a commercial airliner on the inside. I was escorted all the way back to the row just before the last. I felt there had to be a mistake, but I knew there wasn't any chance of reasoning with the officers.

All of the people in the back rows had extra restraints, little black metal boxes were locked over the chain between their handcuffs, forcing them to keep their wrists parallel at all times. The plane was segregated by offense level, length of sentence, or by the security level of the destination prison. I was supposed to be going to a camp, the lowest security level of all the federal prisons, but for some reason I was sat in the back with everyone going to the ADX or the USP.

An officer buckled me into a port side seat on the aisle. Sitting next to me was a very serious looking white man with a completely shaved head and a light brown goatee. He slowly turned his head towards me and then made a show of looking down at my hands, signaling that he had noticed that I was not black boxed. Then he gave me a look that, while I couldn't be sure, resembled 'the accusing eye', the one I had seen so many others get in county jail when people found out that they had snitched on someone or helped the government set someone up in an attempt to get a reduced sentence.

I didn't want him to assume that I was getting this 'special treatment' because I had snitched or cooperated, which is just about the worst thing you can have a reputation for in this crowd, and I felt pressured to lighten the mood, so I looked at him and said what first came to my mind, "Has anyone ever told you that you look just like Cyrus the Virus?"

Keeping his gaze forward to convey that I wasn't worth directly addressing, he responded with a calm yet unnaturally deep voice. "All the time." I realized talking might not be the best thing at this point.

I closed my eyes and tried to teleport myself somewhere else. I caught a flash of the faded past, when I first met Buzz Aldrin. I was pissing in a urinal and he just walked up and used the one next to me. I had always wanted to meet him, to ask him a million questions, but now he was right there and I couldn't ask him anything.

I open my eyes and found myself back on Con Air with Cyrus the Virus, shackled, bleeding a little from my ankles, wondering if I was going to be able to hold my bladder until the next time I saw a toilet, yet worrying that the people surrounding me were thinking that I was getting 'special treatment' because I wasn't black boxed.

Two officers sat behind me in the last row. One of them leaned forward and said, "Hey, professor, is it true you stole moon rocks?" I looked slightly back at him and didn't confirm or deny. It wasn't a good thing to have the cops talking to you.

He pressed forward. "Will you sign this for my wife?" He was holding a post card with the moon on it.

I could feel Cyrus getting agitated so I faced the officer and said, "It's been a long time since I've flown a plane." I raised my cuffs as proof of my claim. "So if you can get me to the copilot's seat and let me fly for just one minute you can have my autograph." That comment safely and effectively ended our conversation.

. . .

The water was cold and the pressure was way too high. We tried to block the attack with our hands, to spread it out a bit, but its bite still hurt.

"Turn around," the officer commanded as he continued to hose us down. Ten of us were standing in a tiled shower, naked and barefoot. The water stopped and the officer started squirting us with a spray bottle glancing a little too long at our penises.

"Rub it all over," he ordered. We followed instructions and then got blasted again.

. . .

The phones in the county jails didn't allow me to call her number, so I didn't expect these phones to work, but it was worth a try. I picked up the receiver and dialed, holding my breath. It rang four times and then I heard her soft voice.

"Hello?" she said.

The machine cut her off and started with its message. "This call is from a Federal Prison. If you wish to accept this call press five now... if you wish to block this call press seven."

I heard the sound of a pushed button.

The computer voice said, "Are you sure you want to block this call? If yes, press seven."

I quickly hung up. I was breathing fast and my hands were sweating. I looked around the room and then began redialing. I had heard her voice. Did she really try to block my call? I had to try again.

It only rang once this time before she picked up. "Hello," she said in her soft and lovely way.

"This call is from a Federal Prison. If you wish to accept this call press five now... if you wish to block this call..." I heard the button being pushed.

"Hello?" she said, checking to see if we were able to talk now.

"Hi," I replied.

"I'm so sorry," she said. "I didn't hear it very well the first time and thought it said to push seven."

I melted, holding the phone to my face with both hands and sighing. Everything I had prepared for this moment, the words I had carefully selected and practiced for over a year completely escaped me. "It's really really good to hear your voice," I said.

"Its good to hear your voice too," she said. "How are you doing?" she asked.

"I'm still alive," I said. "How are you?"

"I don't get out much," she said. "They have me wearing this stupid ankle monitor, so I can't leave the house without permission. It totally sucks."

"How long do you have to wear that?" I asked.

"Up to three more months," she replied.

There was a pause and then I said, "Tiffany…"

My throat was choking up.

"Yeah?" she said.

I closed my eyes, remembering how hot the air was as we ran in a Clear Lake park. I ran so fast, determined to keep her pace. Then, for the first time, she slowed down. I stopped and waited for her. She was holding her side and said, "I don't feel normal. I just don't think I have the energy today." We walked holding hands through the park, letting our hearts slow back down. Just before we looped back to her car she stopped, looked into my eyes and said, "I'm late." We held each other tightly. We didn't talk about how we wanted to respond to this news, we didn't talk about how neither of us really wanted kids, we just held each other affirming that no matter what came our way we would deal with it together.

I opened my eyes and said, "I just got a hundred months."

"I know," she said as she started to cry.

The sound of her crying made my throat swell up more, making it harder to talk. "If you need to move on," I said, "I understand."

"What are you saying?" she said in a quiet choked up voice.

I took a deep breath and tried to talk calmly. "I'm just saying that… well I want you to be happy above all else and I'm going to be gone for a long time. I don't want to be the reason you miss out on life."

After a short pause she said, "Okay, but you know me... I don't really date much anyway." We cried together for a bit.

Another inmate picked up the phone next to me and started to dial. I turned away from him, wiped my tears and tried to clear up my uncooperative throat.

Tiffany pushed past her tears and said, "They really were serious in the court room."

"Yeah, no kidding," I replied.

"I don't get it," she added. "I mean, it's not like we were murders or even drug dealers."

I started to laugh, imaging how her face had moved as she said those words.

"I can't believe you made me laugh right now," I said.

"Seriously," she added, "the way they talked... it was like they thought we were really bad people."

I relaxed. After all of this time I didn't expect to hear her talk like this. I didn't even know if she was going to take the call.

"So what's it like in there," she asked.

I began telling her random stories about the crazy people I've seen, but thought it was best to avoid telling her about any of the violence.

"You have one minute," the computer voice interrupted.

"Thanks for giving your phone number to my lawyer," I said.

She was quiet. "We don't have much time and I really need a way to stay in touch with you. No matter what happens, wherever your life goes, whatever I have to go through in here, I can survive it all as long as I have a way to communicate with you."

"I don't know," she said. "They told me I'm not supposed to communicate with you anymore."

"I don't think they can legally force you to not communicate with someone," I said.

"My lawyer, the prosecutor, my house arrest officer, they all told me that," she said.

I knew they were all lying to her, but I also knew that she didn't know they were lying to her. I leaned forward, worried that the phone was going to cut off.

"Well then can you at least give me an address so that I can send you letters?" I asked.

She hesitated and then gave me her sister's address.

I repeated it out loud, but didn't have anything to write it down with.

"If you're really worried about sending me letters, you can always have a friend of yours send me post cards. Even blank ones," I suggested.

The phone beeped twice.

"Are you still there?" I asked.

"Yes," she said.

"I love you Tiffany," I said.

"I love you too," she said. The call timed out and was over.

I walked quickly to my cell, wrote down the address she gave me, and spent all night writing poetry.

The cells were completely different. The doors were made out of wood, with little glass windows in them. There were no food slots. The toilets were made of porcelain, with seats, and the sink was a separate entity, also made of porcelain, with hot and cold knobs that twisted on and off instead of needing to be pumped just right to start to trickle. The bunk bed was similar to what I had become used to, but the walls were clean, as if their entire building was new. It felt luxurious.

The doors popped open. My bunky jumped up and left the room. He was a broad shouldered black man, with a shaved head. He hadn't said much to me since I arrived last night.

I exited the cell and began to explore my new domain. It was much larger than the pods I had seen before. Two floors, thirty cells on each, two TV rooms, controlled by the officers, so there was no fighting over what was going to be watched. Walking around the perimeter took more than four times longer than my last perimeter routine.

"What's up?" a young slender white kid said as he approached me.

"Not much," I said. "I just arrived last night."

"Just arrested, or come from County?" he asked.

"County," I said.

"Oh," he replied, "well let me give you the break down. Wednesdays for lunch we get hamburgers, real hamburgers, and Thursdays we get chicken for dinner." He leaned in close and whispered, "Tonight!" with excited eyes. "And for breakfasts we get eggs of some kind like every third day. Way better than in County."

His body language said that he was telling the truth, but I found his claims hard to believe.

"My name is Pat," he said as he stretched out his hand. I shook it, and said, "I'm Thad."

"What are you into?" he asked.

"What do you mean?" I said.

"You know, sports, girls, science, crochet... what do you like to do?"

I paused for a moment and then said, "I just realized that its been a really long time since anybody has asked me anything like that." He waited patiently for my answer.

I tried to recall a life that made such questions possible. "Girls, physics, astronomy, geology, flying, SCUBA diving, hiking, philosophy, mining..." He was still looking at me like he was paying attention.

"Great," he said. "I've been dying to have an actual intellectual conversation with someone. We sat at one of the tables and lost hours talking about dark energy, the Many Worlds Interpretation of quantum mechanics, time travel, consciousness, and evolution.

"I ain't come from no monkey," an inmate said, rudely cutting into our conversation. He stood up to assert this, apparently thinking that by escalating violence with his claim he somehow bolstered it.

"What did you come from then?" Pat asked, dying for him to actually engage in real debate.

"I ain't come from no monkey, I tell you dat," he repeated.

"You're right," I said. "None of us came from monkeys." He seemed happy with this. I continued, "We came from apes, great apes to be specific. Humans are great apes. Our parents are great apes, and we are great apes."

"I ain't come from no ape neither," he said. "I ain't no animal."

"Well then," Pat asked, "if you're not an animal, please tell me, are you a Plant, Fungus, Protista, or Bacteria?" The inmate stomped off muttering.

We continued our conversation until dinner.

"Chow time! Chow time! Chow time!" the pod officer yelled.

Everyone got in line. "Oh God I can't wait," Pat said. "I need like three thousand calories a day to stay well, and that's hard to do in here you know?" The officer handed me a tray. I couldn't believe my eyes. It wasn't just chicken, it was an entire crispy baked leg quarter, diced potatoes, green beans, and a roll.

"Holy shit!" I said.

"Told you," Pat replied. We searched for an open table and sat down. I ate the green beans first, then slowly savored each potato. Then I pulled the chicken in half and put a small piece in my mouth. I closed my eyes and started making sounds of pleasure.

"Stop it," Pat said jokingly. "People will think someone's under the table giving you a blow job or something." I made each bite last as long as I could. Then I picked up the leg and put it on Pat's tray.

"You sure?" he asked.

"You said you need the extra calories," I said. "I haven't had this much to eat in over a year."

"Thanks man," he said as he salivated in anticipation. "I won't forget it."

卌 卌 卌 卌 卌 卌 卌 卌 卌 卌 卌 卌 卌 卌
卌 卌 卌 卌 卌 卌 卌 卌 卌 卌 卌 卌 卌 卌
卌 卌 卌 卌 卌 卌 卌 卌 卌 卌 卌 卌 卌 卌
卌 卌 卌 卌 卌 卌 卌 卌 卌 卌 卌 卌 卌 卌
卌 卌 卌 卌 卌 卌 卌 卌 卌 卌 卌 卌 卌 卌
卌 卌 卌 卌 卌 卌 卌 卌 卌 卌 卌 卌 卌 卌
卌 卌 卌 卌 卌 卌 卌 卌 卌 卌 卌 卌 卌 |

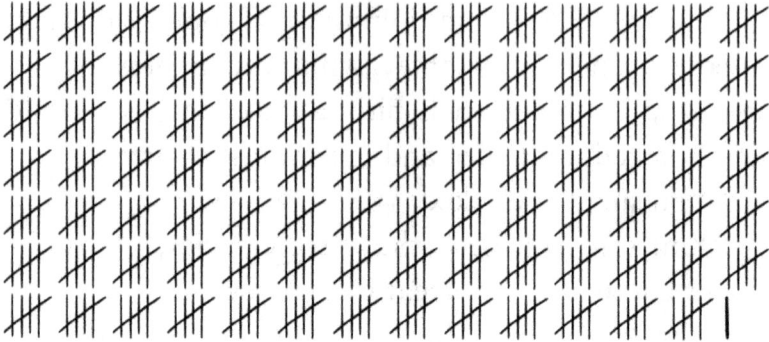

My bunky was standing up, leaning on my bunk with his elbows. "I'm telling you man, she was sucking two monster cocks at the same time."

"You mean one and then the other?" I asked. "Or literally at the same time?"

"The same time man, both of 'em in her mouth down to the balls. Fucking bitch was smokin' too. He looked at me with hesitation and then said, "You ever fucked a fat chick?" I didn't respond. "Cuz I know you white boys likes 'em skinny, but you really should try dem fat chicks, got's more cushion for the pushin'."

"At this point," I said, "I'd be ecstatic for any girl eighteen to ninety-nine."

He took this as an invitation to share another one of his sex stories.

"Let me tell ya 'bout dem old bitches," he said. "Dey ain't messin' around. Go right for it, lay it all out der, dey is serious 'bout that dick." He was grinning ear to ear. "One time I hooked up with this bitch in her sixties, barely got in the door and she was down on her muthafuckin' knees pulling my pants down and stuffing her face. Hot as shit nigga." He shook his hand making his finger slap against the others to emphasize his words. After twenty more minutes of storytelling he sunk into his bunk. I closed my eyes and tried to fall asleep.

A few minutes later I felt the vibration and heard the slurping sounds of a wet hand. I pretended to be asleep. A few minutes into it he got out of bed, walked over to the toilet, pulled his pants down to his ankles and started stroking much more vigorously. A minute later he shot a large load into the bowl and let out a sigh. He wasn't really trying to be quiet. I was on my side, facing his way, trying not to move.

...

"Damn right I killed him," my new bunky said. "Ain't no way I'm gonna let that fuck keep breathing as long as my sister is alive."

"So then why didn't they charge you with murder?" I asked.

"Look, my sister used to be married to this dude, said the vows, all that. Then he starts drinking and she starts showing up to my place to stay the night with bruises all over her. She keeps going back to him, thinking it's gonna somehow get better, but every time he drinks he uses her as a punching bag, know what I'm saying?"

"I eventually get her to divorce his ass, help her get into a new place, even get a restraining order against him. Then she tells me that he's been showing up outside her house, talk'n 'bout 'let me in, I just want to talk,' all drunk and shit. So I tell her to sleep at my place and I go over to hers for the night. Sure as shit, he shows up clawing at the bedroom window. I left it unlocked, kept the lights off, and waited as he climbed in. Soon as he was inside I snapped on the lights, sitting there calm and shit with my shotgun pointed at him. Told him straight up, 'Tonight you're gonna die, do you want to talk about it, say some words and shit, or get it over right now?' We talked about it for a while and then he sat there, by the window and I got up and shot him right in the head."

"Are you saying that because he was trespassing they didn't charge you with murder?"

"Damn straight. He broke in with the intention to cause harm. Got what's coming to him."

"Well then why are you in here?" I asked.

" 'Cause the God damn shotgun was sawed off. Got me fucked up over cutting my own damn barrel."

· · ·

"Trays!" the CO yelled. I was sitting on the porcelain throne in my cell after lunch, taking my time. A minute later the CO yelled more vigorously. "Trays, trays, trays!" I drifted back off into my trance. A few minutes later the pod officer opened the door to my room, looked around for the missing tray and then on his way out he said, "Sorry man."

After I finished I went back to our usual spot. "What's on your mind?" Pat asked. "Come on, spit it out," he said looking at my face.

"Its just that… the officer just came into my cell while I was shitting and…"

"And what?" he asked.

"Well, he apologized to me."

"So?" Pat said.

"Its just, it hadn't even occurred to me that's all. I hadn't been treated like a human in so long I forgot that it was an option."

"Things will get better," he said. "You'll see. After all, we're off to prison." He smiled in full knowledge of the irony of his statement.

"As long as they have hamburger Wednesdays and chicken Thursdays," I said.

"You wrote her another sonnet?" he asked looking at the paper in my hands.

"Yes, but I'm not done with it yet," I said.

卌 卌 卌 卌 卌 卌 卌 卌 卌 卌 卌 卌 卌 卌
卌 卌 卌 卌 卌 卌 卌 卌 卌 卌 卌 卌 卌 卌
卌 卌 卌 卌 卌 卌 卌 卌 卌 卌 卌 卌 卌 卌
卌 卌 卌 卌 卌 卌 卌 卌 卌 卌 卌 卌 卌 卌
卌 卌 卌 卌 卌 卌 卌 卌 卌 卌 卌 卌 卌 卌
卌 卌 卌 卌 卌 卌 卌 卌 卌 卌 卌 卌 卌 卌
卌 卌 卌 卌 卌 卌 卌 卌 卌 卌 卌 卌 卌 卌
卌 卌

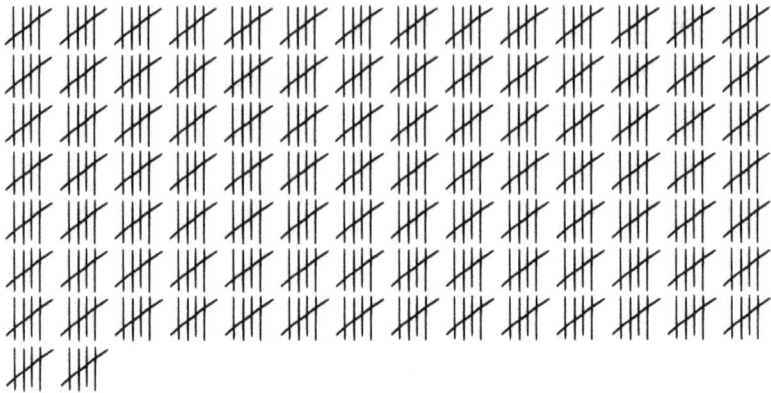

It was dark when we landed. I tried to memorize every turn as the van drove us into the middle of nowhere, to commit every detail to memory, but I couldn't see much and I had no idea how much further we had to go.

The officers removed our handcuffs and then shuffled us into a cement holding cell, leaving us there for the night. I had completely lost my voice. I didn't feel particularly sick, no symptoms of a cold or flu, but my voice was gone. I couldn't even whisper.

"This is it," one of the inmates next to me said in the morning. The sound of keys announced what was coming. "Prison! Ready or not."

Go to www.moonrockbook.com to watch for the next book in this series, schedule the author for a speaking event, join the education movement, and more.

ACKNOWLEDGEMENTS

Under the insight that adversity makes the story, I would like to thank all of the individuals that ended up in the pages of this book. From the puritanical federal judge, to the psychotic thug preachers, the unnecessarily vengeful officials, and the lovers that so deeply cut me—thank you for exposing me to the cold darkness of insecurity and loneliness, texturing me with layers of anguish that inspired a complete reassessment of my life. Climbing out of that abyss has led to growth that has become invaluable to me.

I warmly thank everyone that contributed to the making of this book, for every constructive comment and candid question. A special thanks goes out to: John Gilbert—for his detailed and thoughtful review, which significantly improved the flow of this work, Jamie Lombardi—for being a constant spring of inspiration in my life, and for laboriously working to bring out the nuanced flavor and emotional depth of these real life characters, Angela Arvizu—for her unbounded support and compassion, Dave Nugent—for that gratis winter in Boulder where I wrote down the beginnings of this book, and to Laura de Robles, Karen Tschorn, Andrew Martin Hogstein, David Heggli, Jonathan Farkasofsky, Dwayne Burks and Laura Williams—whose collective criticisms have polished many of the book's rough edges. I also thank Jeff Chapple, Derek Meik and Jamie Lombardi for designing the cover.

ABOUT THE AUTHOR

Thad Roberts is a theoretical physicist, philosopher, and adventurer who passionately explores the possibility that quantum mechanics is not exact, but instead, is an accurate approximation of a deeper deterministic theory. His research shines a spotlight on the virtues of quantum space theory—a pilot-wave theory that explains the phenomena of general relativity and quantum mechanics in terms of the interactive geometry of the vacuum—an idea that Nobel laureate Louis de Broglie called, "the most natural proposal of all." Thad explores the beauty of this model in his groundbreaking book *Einstein's Intuition: Visualizing Nature in Eleven Dimensions.*

Thad has excavated dinosaur fossils, sailed across two oceans in a 55' sloop, and lived out of a VW Vanagon for 2 years while traveling the world on $10 a day. He has worked as an astrophysicist for NASA, and a flight lead—training astronauts for their space walks. His life took an infamous twist when, to impress a girl, he stole the moon, or moon rocks—a story that is captured in the best-selling book *Sex on the Moon* by Ben Mezrich, which sets the stage for this book.

Today, in addition to his physics work, Thad is the COO of a start up company set to change its industry, and a motivational speaker for the American Program Bureau. He is an adventure photographer, pilot, drone enthusiast, and traveler—and he is still making plans to go to space.

www.ingramcontent.com/pod-product-compliance
Lightning Source LLC
Chambersburg PA
CBHW072112270326
41931CB00010B/1538